THE BEATLES CLICHÉS

Whether you love them or hate them!

THE BEATLES CLICHÉS
Erick Falc'her-Poyroux

Hope you like this
little book and ...
enjoy the music!

Erick F. P.

AMERGIN BOOKS

To Lann & Tifenn, once again!

Thanks to Yannick Falc'her for the musical initiation.

Thanks to my parents Jo & Serge Poyroux for a home full of music of every kind.

Thanks to Justina for her patience and love.

Additional thanks for proof-reading to Justina, once more, as well as to Nick Grundy and Sarah Joksimovic.

THE ORIGINS

THE MUSIC

THE END

ADDITIONAL INFORMATION

About the Author

Erick Falc'her-Poyroux

 Born in Nantes, France, on a snowy Monday morning in January 1964 – a couple of days before The Beatles début in Versailles, near Paris – he was given his first Beatles album by his uncle at the age of 10. Slightly perplexed, he asked for a pair of walkie-talkies instead. By 13, the magic had finally worked and he abandoned his collection of tree leaves to start a new one, consisting of Beatles recordings.

Nowadays, and to a large extent thanks to John, Paul, George and Ringo, he is a Senior Lecturer at the University of Nantes, France, where he is the head of the language department in the graduate school of engineering. He is also the author of a Ph.D. thesis on the identity of Irish music (university Rennes II, 1996) and of several books on Ireland.

BEATLES (The) - English musical group formed in Liverpool, consisting, between August 1962 and April 1970, of John Lennon (1940 -1980), Paul McCartney (born 1942), George Harrison (1943 -2001) and Richard Starkey (a.k.a. Ringo Starr, born 1940).

After discovering Elvis Presley, John created his first band The Quarry Men in 1956, joined by Paul in 1957, then by George in 1958. In 1960, Peter Best and Stuart Sutcliffe joined the group to play in Hamburg strip clubs, where they took the name of The Beatles.

In 1961, Stuart chose to remain and live in Hamburg and Brian Epstein became their manager after seeing them play at the Cavern, their local club in Liverpool. In 1962, they signed a contract with Parlophone (an EMI subsidiary), Peter was replaced by Ringo, and their first single, "Love Me Do" reached number 17 in the UK charts. The Beatles became a phenomenon in Great Britain in late 1963, and a triumphant visit to the U.S.A in early 1964 confirmed their international status.

Between 1962 and 1970, they released 12 albums in Britain (11 of which became number 1), 22 singles (including 17 reaching number 1) and 13 EPs, under the guidance of their producer George Martin. They stopped touring in August 1966 to devote themselves solely to studio work. In 1967, their manager Brian Epstein died and the following year they created their own company – Apple – to run their businesses.

The first musical and personal differences became more obvious around this period and in September 1969, John announced to the other 3 members that he was leaving the band. He agreed however not to disclose the information for a few months. Paul confirmed the separation to the public on April 10, 1970 in a press statement whilst announcing his first solo album.

John was killed on Dec. 8, 1980 and George died of cancer on Nov. 29, 2001. Paul was knighted by the Queen in 1997, followed by Ringo in 2018, and EMI continues to publish unreleased recordings and compilations of the band, with enduring success.

Introduction

The Beatles, New York airport, February 7, 1964

The Beatles were a musical comet in the sky of the twentieth century, the effects of which can still be felt today. Not a day goes by without hearing their songs in the media, not a year without seeing them in the headlines, not a decade without a major musical event involving their music.

Regarded by some as a glorious example to look up to, and by others as over-rated peddlers of soppiness, they rarely leave anyone indifferent. But, whether you love or hate The Beatles, everyone thinks they know them through their music and the image reflected by the media: the "Four Lads from Liverpool", the hysteria of the early days of Beatlemania, the 'moptop' hairstyle, the rivalry with the Rolling Stones, the childlike chorus of "Yellow Submarine", the psychedelic jackets, etc. Not to mention the irruption of Yoko Ono, the never-ending trials, and in 1980 the assassination of John Lennon that put a final end to the dreams of a reunion. But none of this can account for their impressive popularity, fifty years on.

Of course, collectors keep on accumulating and musicians keep on emulating. But very few books have taken a simple look at what people believe about them, few documents have simply tried to look slightly beyond the image we all know. Over the last decades, however, a useful stream of writings has emerged, looking with renewed interest at the career of the "Fab Four" (their most common nickname). Since the mid 1990s (and most probably because of the 1995 television series *Anthology*, along with a major reference book in 2000), researchers in musicology have started considering this musical and social phenomenon as worthy of study: some books or documentaries analyse in detail the composition talents of the group, while others shed light on the multiple social and political implications of The Beatles' music, and still more volumes bring to our attention the questions of identity raised by the band during the post baby-boom period. With passion and conviction, all these researchers, most of whom were barely born at the dawn of Beatlemania, help us better understand the cultural and musical revolution associated with The Beatles during the sixties, in no small part thanks to the filtering perspective brought by the 50 years that have passed since their separation.

This little book will certainly not attempt to explain everything you need to know about what was, after all, "*just a band who made it very, very big*" as John Lennon put it in 1970. More modestly, the objective of the chapters that follow is to disentangle facts and rumours, to recognize history from mythology, sometimes created by The Beatles themselves, and to restore certain facts too often forgotten. Starting from what everyone knows, or what everyone *assumes* they know, we will concentrate on the main episodes of their story, and review their careers.

And hopefully, if some of our readers only learn a little more about their pre-existing passion, others might even take a liking to it.

01 - "The Beatles were working-class heroes."

"A working-class hero is something to be"
John Lennon, "Working Class Hero", 1970

Liverpool, a city-port established at the beginning of the 18th century, is a major trading centre in Europe, suffering from a negative image as an industrial city despite its cosmopolitan character. Having witnessed a large influx of Irish immigrants in the mid-19th century, driven into exile by the Great Famine, the population of Liverpool peaked in the early 20th century along with the activity of its ports, before declining after the First World War. In 1960, the city still had about 700,000 inhabitants (compared to only 498,000 in 2019) and its industrial character still dominated.

It was in this context that the four members of the group were born between 1940 and 1943. Three of them, Paul, John and George, have acknowledged their Irish origins and McCartney never fails to recall that "*Liverpool, they used to call it the 'Capital of Ireland'*" (*All You Need Is Love, The Story of Popular Music*, 1977). He even went as far as writing in his poem *Irish Language*: "*The Beatles were a bunch of Micks*".

One of the main advantages of a city like Liverpool in the 50s and 60s was therefore its direct link with the rest of the world through maritime trade, and more specifically with the United States and its musical production. All the musicians in Liverpool knew at least someone from whom they could buy the latest singles by some of their idols, such as Elvis, Chet Atkins, Big Bill Broonzy, Buddy Holly, and the Everly Brothers.

A whole generation thus immersed itself in music with a rare passion, giving birth in the mid-1960s to a wave of artists from Liverpool, later dubbed by the media the "Mersey Beat", after the river that flows through the city.

Ringo Starr, born on July 7, 1940, is – out of the four Beatles – probably the one who grew up in the poorest neighbourhood, at 10 Admiral Grove, which he remembers in his song *Y Not* (2010): "*The other side of Liverpool is cold and damp ... you just had to laugh*".("The Other Side of Liverpool").

Contrary to a well-known cliché – after all, he wrote the song "Working Class Hero"– John Lennon came from a middle-class neighbourhood. Born on October 9, 1940, he was raised from the age of 9 by his Aunt Mimi on Menlove Avenue, a residential neighbourhood south of the city, where his mother was run over and killed by a car in July 1958.

Menlove Avenue

Forthlin Road

Two kilometres from Menlove, at 12 Forthlin Road, stands the small house where Paul McCartney grew up. Born on June 18, 1942, he also lost his mother as a teenager. And like John Lennon's, his house was later bought by the National Trust (the British heritage institution) and turned into a museum.

Finally, George Harrison, born on February 25, 1943, also grew up in a very modest house, at 12 Arnold Grove, and was only admitted in the band at the age of 15, thanks to the insistence of his school-friend Paul.

The origin of The Beatles' music is thus to be found in this then-new urban tradition called Rock'n'Roll, and its toned down British counterpart, Skiffle. The Quarry Men (named after the school attended by John Lennon, the Quarry Bank High School), was the first band created by John Lennon in 1956, which became the Silver Beatles in 1960, before being simply abridged to The Beatles. This play on words between "beetle" and "beat" appears to be credited as much to John as to his friend Stuart Sutcliffe, the bassist of the group between 1960 and 1961. George explained in 1995 the possible dual origin of the name: "*There was the Crickets who backed Buddy Holly, that similarity. But Stuart was really into Marlon Brando, and in the movie The Wild One, there is a scene where Lee Marvin (Chino) says: 'Johnny, we've been looking for you, the Beetles* [a rival gang of bikers] *have missed you.*" (*Anthology*).

It was also in 1960 that the group found its first real drummer, Pete Best, the son of the owner of a Liverpool music club, the Casbah. He remained faithful to The Beatles until August 1962, before being ousted at the request of producer George Martin after their first audition, simply because he did not find him good enough for the job. It didn't take long for the three other members to find a replacement, in Ringo. It is true that Pete naturally displayed a certain melancholy, while their new drummer – whom they already knew very well from the Liverpool music scene and the long nights in Hamburg – was notorious for his sense of humour, in addition to his musical skills.

Considered a bleak industrial region, northern England was long neglected and ignored by the south of the country (and sometimes still is!), which largely explains the difficulties The Beatles came up against when looking for a recording contract in 1962 in London. It took all the strength of character of their manager Brian Epstein to find a deal for his protégés, after discovering them in 1961 playing in the Cavern, the Liverpool club where the story really started. From the very beginning, he had decided to play down the humble origins of the band, so as to aim for the widest possible audience the world over: "*They have been called a working-class phenomenon*", he explained during a press conference in New York in November 1963, "*but I disagree with the sometimes expressed notion that their appeal is sometimes to the working classes. The Beatles are classless.*"

Throughout their career, the Fab Four consistently showed a strong attachment to their hometown through their songs, from "In My Life" (on *Rubber Soul*, 1965) to "Maggie Mae" (on *Let It Be*, 1970) and of course with the single released in February 1967: "Penny Lane / Strawberry Fields Forever". "Penny Lane" composed by Paul, is clearly nostalgic ("*Penny Lane is in my ears and in my eyes, there beneath the blue suburban skies*") and conjures up the characters living in a familiar neighbourhood: "*They're both songs about Liverpool as well... a lot of our formative years were spent walking around those places. Penny Lane was the depot I had to change buses at to get from my house to John's and to a lot of my friends.*" (Paul, *Anthology*, 1995). The second song, composed by John, recalls the garden of a local orphanage where he used to play as a child, with a more personal approach: "*We were trying to write about Liverpool, and I just listed all the nice-sounding names arbitrarily. But I have visions of Strawberry Fields.... Because Strawberry Fields is just anywhere you want to go.*" (John, *Rolling Stone*, 1968).

It has often been pointed out that The Beatles left Liverpool for London early in their career, which is true. But it is equally correct to consider that they have consistently championed their geographical origins, in spite of the distance: this was the case in particular in 1991 when Paul composed his first classical work, the "Liverpool Oratorio", a symbol of his attachment to his native city, where, in 1996, he also founded the Liverpool Institute for Performing Arts in the buildings of his childhood school. This was again the case in 2008 when Ringo released a single and an album called "Liverpool 8"named after the neighbourhood where he grew up: "*Liverpool, I left you, but I never let you down*".

In contrast, only John Lennon can be said to have had a real interest in politics, albeit brief. We can of course find traces of this in some of his songs like "Working Class Hero"or "Instant Karma", both in 1970: "*Why in the world are we here? / Surely not to live in pain and fear / Why on earth are you there? When you're everywhere, come and get your share*".

But Lennon himself conceded in one of his last major interviews: "*I dabbled in so-called politics in the late '60s and '70s more out of guilt than anything. Guilt for being rich, and guilt thinking that perhaps love and peace isn't enough and you have to go and get shot or something, or get punched in the face, to prove I'm one of the people. I was doing it against my instincts.*" (*Playboy* interview, 1980).

Few cities are therefore as clearly associated with a band as Liverpool is with The Beatles, and vice versa. Paul McCartney once explained without hesitation: "*I've been right around the world a few times, to all its little pockets; and, in truth, I'd swear to God I've never met any people more soulful, more intelligent, more kind, more filled with common sense than the people I came from in Liverpool*" (*Playboy* interview, 1984). And maybe it was precisely this down-to-earth attitude, as well as the cynical humour unique to the

14

Liverpool area that helped the Fab Four keep a cool head during the wildest years of their career.

Yet, for a long time the city ignored the impact of the group and its cultural significance: it did not hesitate for example to demolish the famous Cavern club in 1973 and replace it with a car park, before rebuilding a replica in 1984 in response to pressure from the media and the public. It wasn't until 1990 that a museum worthy of their name was established on the waterfront, The Beatles Story. By contrast, the city today seems peppered with reminders of the band, and in particular with statues: Eleanor Rigby, the heroine of the 1966 McCartney song, has been sitting alone on her bench since 1982, while John Lennon's statue has been leaning against the wall opposite the new Cavern since 1997, and their four statues - designed by Liverpool artist Andy Edwards - have been strutting on the Pier Head since 2015. A replica of the Yellow Submarine from the 1968 animated feature has also been on display since 1984, the airport was named the John Lennon Airport in 2002, the luxury hotel in the city centre was named the "Hard Day's Night" in 2004, July 10th was officially declared "Beatles Day" by the municipality in 2008 and, by way of consecration, the Liverpool Hope University started offering a Master's degree dedicated to The Beatles in 2009.

Beatles statues on Pier Head (photo R. Winter)

The Beatles in Hamburg

*"I didn't grow up in Liverpool.
I grew up in Hamburg"*
John Lennon 1971.

Another country, another port: it was in Hamburg between August 1960 and December 1962, over the course of five stays, that The Beatles forged the powerful and eclectic style that they developed throughout their career.

Recruited by a German impresario looking for English bands, they initially spent nearly four months in one of the most infamous red light districts in Europe, at a time when George Harrison was only 17 years old. And it was precisely for this reason that they were expelled by the authorities in December 1960: "*All the club owners were like gangsters, and all the waiters had tear-gas guns, truncheons, knuckle-dusters. They were a heavy crew. Everybody around that district were homosexuals, pimps, hookers. You know, being in the middle of that when I was 17. It was good fun*" (George Harrison, *Crawdaddy*, February 1977).

The Beatles in Hamburg (Indra Club, August 1960)

Back in Hamburg in April 1961, after George's eighteenth birthday, they became local stars in the best clubs of the same shady neighbourhood, the Top Ten and the Star Club. Thanks to these contracts, The Beatles began to earn a living and to learn their craft, playing all kinds of music in very different styles for a demanding but distracted audience, mostly made up of sailors and businessmen. They generally performed for long sessions at night, from 7.30 pm to 2.30 am, seven days a week, drawing their energy from the Preludin pills kindly provided by the service lady, Rosa Hoffman.

The impact of this intense period on their stage performances was almost immediate in Liverpool. In the 1963 BBC documentary *Mersey Sound*, George explained: *"We'd been to Hamburg. I think that's where we found our style... we developed our style because of this fellow. He used to say, 'You've got to make a show for the people.' And he used to come up every night, shouting 'Mach schau! Mach schau!' So we used to 'mach schau', and John used to dance around like a gorilla, and we'd all, you know, knock our heads together and things like that. Anyway, we got back to Liverpool and all the groups there were doing 'Shadows' type of stuff. And we came back with leather jackets and jeans and funny hair – 'maching schau' - which went down quite well.*

They eventually signed a recording contract with Polydor in Germany to accompany British singer Tony Sheridan, notably on a rocked-up version of the traditional British song "My Bonnie": it was this recording that eventually reached the ears of Brian Epstein, head of a record store in Liverpool, and pushed him to meet them and to become their manager.

During this period, they also met young German students close to the existentialist movement, including Klaus Voorman, Jürgen Vollmer and Astrid Kirchherr. It was Astrid who helped them develop their image through her extraordinary artistic skills as a photographer, her taste for fashion and her interest in hairdressing (she is sometimes credited with the invention of The Beatles 'moptop' haircut). The film *Backbeat* (1992) recounts this period and traces the true story of Stuart Sutcliffe, The Beatles' original bass player who decided in 1961 to leave the band to live with Astrid and devote himself exclusively to his passion for painting. Sadly, he died of a brain haemorrhage on April 10th 1962.

Their last three stays in Hamburg in 1962, a sonic evidence of which can be found on a recording published in 1977, saw their status

02 – "the Rolling Stones were the real rebels."

"Their success in America broke down a lot of doors that helped everyone else from England that followed."
Mick Jagger, 1988.

The rivalry between The Beatles and the Rolling Stones is one of the most widespread and enduring clichés in the history of Rock music. In this well-established pattern, The Beatles are regarded as gentle pop stars revered by girls, and the Rolling Stones are the real Rock rebels, slightly more popular with boys.

In the British context of the 1960s, this contrast was perfectly understandable, in parallel with the opposition between Mods and Rockers: from 1964 to 1966, violent clashes were frequent between these rival social groups, representing two divergent lifestyles. Whereas Mods sought sophistication and simplicity, Rockers saw themselves as leather-clad rebels. This phenomenon was even alluded to in The Beatles' first movie, *A Hard Day's Night* (1964): when a journalist asks Ringo whether he is a Mod or a Rocker, he replies: "I'm a *mocker!*".

But in reality, this apparent contrast between The Beatles and the Rolling Stones was first and foremost the product of brilliant marketing work by the Rolling Stones' first manager and producer, Andrew Loog Oldham. The band, formed in London in 1962 around Mick Jagger and Keith Richards, was first spotted in early 1963 by Oldham, who had previously worked with Brian Epstein, The Beatles' manager. Thanks to his contacts, the Rolling Stones' second single (the raw and energetic "I Wanna Be Your Man") was written for them by Lennon/McCartney, at a time when the Rolling Stones did not compose their own songs yet. Learning their lesson, they quickly drew their inspiration from the example of Lennon and McCartney to fashion their own repertoire... and boost their profit.

It was also thanks to The Beatles' recommendations – and in particular to George Harrison who had seen the Rolling Stones play at the Crawdaddy Club in Richmond, Surrey – that Decca decided to sign them up. Having missed a golden opportunity in January 1962 by refusing The Beatles, it didn't take long for Dick Rowe and Edward Lewis to offer the Rolling Stones a contract. After some hesitation as to what band image might work best commercially, Loog Oldham's genius was to unconsciously sense the potential market of rivalry and to focus his communication on the differences with The Beatles in order to clearly mark his band's territory, with obvious commercial benefits. Thus, from the band's first American tour in May 1964, press releases trumpeted loud and clear that the band was *"dirtier and streakier and more disheveled than The Beatles"*. It was also Loog Oldham who coined the provocative slogan *"Would you let your daughter marry a Rolling Stone?"*. He later explained in the New Musical Express magazine: *"I unconsciously understood that if The Beatles were successful, another section of the audience would seek their opposites"* (1971). In fairness, Loog Oldham was also taking advantage of a rather natural inclination of his *protégés*, particularly Mick Jagger, who could grin and pull faces at will, refused to wear a suit on stage, wore slightly longer hair, etc., while at the same time seeming more accessible to the general public.

But the English-speaking media were more interested in the private lives of the group's members, particularly the inevitable arrests of Jagger and Richards in 1967 for possession of drugs. It would be some time before Lennon fell on the same charges (1968), and then Harrison (1969), who explained that *"There was a kind of social pecking order that was in the pop world. First they busted Donovan (...), then they busted the Rolling Stones, and then they worked their way up and they busted John and Yoko, and me"*.

Musically, it was obvious that the two bands had chosen relatively different paths as early as 1964: if the Rolling Stones came from the Rhythm'n'Blues scene and have remained firmly in their tracks for decades despite a few escapades (the band's name comes from a Muddy Waters song), The Beatles were always looking to surprise their audience by constantly experimenting with different styles and influences. The contrast was also unmistakable during the early period (1963-1965) between a band that could write their own songs with titles such as"I Wanna Hold Your Hand" (The Beatles in 1963) and another one that covered Willie Dixon's "I Just Want To Make Love To You" (The Rolling Stones in 1964).

In terms of orchestration, one cannot help but notice that the Rolling Stones also followed The Beatles' example several times, notably by using a sitar on "Paint It Black" (1966), one year after "Norwegian Wood" (1965), or by adding a string orchestra on "As Tears Go By" (written in 1964 but recorded in October 1965), as in "Yesterday" (released in August 1965). John Lennon remarked with a certain degree of malice in 1971: *"I'd like to make a list of all the things we did and that the Stones*

*did two months later.... Satanic Majesties is Pepper.
We Love You is All You Need Is Love... I hate the
implication that the Stones were revolutionaries but
not The Beatles."* (*Rolling Stone* interview).

Turning to the lyrics of the songs, if the first
texts by The Beatles do not demonstrate any
sarcastic quality, those of the Rolling Stones on
the other hand are immediately recognizable by
their aggressiveness, and even by their insolence.
Critics have never failed for example to
underline the misogynistic character of many of
their songs ("Under My Thumb" and "Stupid
Girl" in 1966, "Yesterday's Papers" in 1967),
while forgetting, willingly or not, that Lennon
was no less misogynistic as late as 1966 in "Run
For Your Life", and many more besides.

The fact remains that, from the outset, each of
the four members of The Beatles appealed to the
British Establishment, becoming in a way the
ideal son-in-law for some, and for others the
symbol of an old-fashioned system that needed
to be overthrown. Still, invited to play before the
Queen at the annual Royal Variety Performance
on November 4, 1963, John Lennon could not
refrain from making a cleverly-prepared and
sarcastic remark: *"For our last number, I'd like to
ask for your help. For those in the cheaper seats, clap
your hands. And for the rest of you, just rattle your
jewellery"*. The whole theatre erupted in laughter.

There was nonetheless some disapproval in
June 1965 when it was announced that The
Beatles were to be awarded the prestigious
Member of the British Empire medal by the
Queen. Some celebrities even returned their
decorations at the time, which John dismissed
with a simple remark: *"A lot of people got this
medal for killing people. We got ours for entertaining
them. I think we deserve ours more."* Which didn't
stop him from sending his own medal back to

Buckingham Palace in 1969 with this short ironic note: "*I am returning the M.B.E. in protest against Britain's involvement in the Nigeria-Biafra thing, against our support of America in Vietnam, and against 'Cold Turkey' slipping down the charts*".

Socially and politically, Lennon was always most uncomfortable in the media straightjacket imposed on them by their manager Brian Epstein, willingly indulging in controversial comments: his remarks about Jesus in March 1966 are more than famous ("*Christianity will go. It will vanish and shrink. I needn't argue with that; I'm right and I will be proved right. We're more popular than Jesus now*"), remarks for which he had to apologize in the USA in August 1966 because of the scandal caused ("*I'm not saying we're better or greater, or comparing us with Jesus Christ as a person, or God as a thing or whatever it is (...). If I had said television was more popular than Jesus, I might have got away with it.*")

It was also John Lennon who became the group's spokesman as early as June 1966 on the Vietnam War, declaring in a cautious and measured manner during a press conference: "*we think about it everyday, and we don't agree with it and we think it's wrong. That's how much interest we take. That's all we can do about it... and say that we don't like it.*" Also very vocal on this issue, George explained a few weeks later: "*war is wrong, and it's obvious it's wrong. And that's all that needs to be said about it.*" (August 66).

The 1967/1968 period was particularly rich in contrast, between The Beatles considered as the ambassadors of the Flower Power movement advocating peace and love ("All You Need Is Love", 1967) and the Rolling Stones, apparently adopting a more hard-line stance ("Street

Fighting Man", 1968). While The Beatles had retired to India for several weeks of transcendental meditation with the Maharishi Mahesh Yogi, Mick Jagger was seen marching in the massive demonstration in London on March 17, 1968 against the Vietnam War, definitely winning the favour of the radical left. On the other hand, Lennon's song "Revolution" (August 1968) attracted the wrath of British revolutionaries who saw in it only "*a lamentable petty bourgeois cry of fear*", as the very revolutionary British magazine *New Left Review* wrote, forgetting that the Stones' song was just as ambiguous in its stance on violence.

That year, as British journalist Leo Burley explained, "*there was a feeling on the far left and in the media that the Stones, thanks in part to Jagger's appearance at Grosvenor Square and songs such as "Street Fighting Man" and "Sympathy", were at the vanguard of the struggle against an archaic political system while Lennon and The Beatles, with their OBEs [sic], now belonged to and spoke for the Establishment*" (*The Independent,* March 9th 2008). In retrospect, however, we do know how Mick Jagger ended up quickly abandoning his militant posture, and more importantly how John Lennon became the standard bearer for peace activism with his striking slogans "Give Peace A Chance" (1969) or "Imagine" (1971), whose simplicity has turned these peace anthems into part of the world's cultural heritage.

The opposition created from the beginning between the two bands existed mainly for the communication needs of the Rolling Stones, the members themselves regularly insisting they were in fact close friends and participating in each other's projects: Mick Jagger, for example, participated in the recording of "All You Need Is Love" in June 1967 and John Lennon took part in a TV show entirely imagined by the Rolling Stones in 1968, "Rock'n'Roll Circus" (which wasn't released until 1996!). *"We were like kings of the jungle then, and we were very close to the Stones. I don't know how close the others were but I spent a lot of time with Brian and Mick"* (Lennon, 1970).

Lennon & Richards in 1968

The fact remains that this alleged opposition constructed by the media is emblematic of that pivotal period in the 1960s, when England sought a new social and cultural identity, and when the world surfed in turn on Pop and Rock, on non-violence and rebellion, on reformism and revolution, on love and war. More prosaically, one might recall the opinion of Sean O'Mahony, who was ironically the publisher of both bands' official fan magazines in the 60s: *"The Beatles were thugs who were put across as nice blokes, and the Rolling Stones were gentlemen who were made into thugs by Andrew."*

03 – "Beatlemania was the most incomprehensible phenomenon of the 1960s."

> "*The world used us as an excuse to go mad, and then blamed it on us.*"
> George Harrison, *Anthology*, 1995.

Beatlemania, a phenomenon of intense collective hysteria which appeared around the time of their second album (*With The Beatles*, November 1963), is less striking for its novelty (Sinatra or Elvis had provoked similar reactions) than for its sheer magnitude, as the whole world – or almost – surrendered to the wave in a matter of weeks.

Although the exact date seems difficult to define, the term was probably first coined on October 13, 1963 by the Daily Mirror reporting on The Beatles' first chaotic appearance on the big television show "Sunday Night At The London Palladium", or on November 1st of the same year when, returning from a tour of Sweden, they were greeted by thousands of teenage girls at London airport.

As early as November, American journalists from CBS, ABC and NBC had started reporting on the phenomenon on the other side of the Atlantic. Brian Epstein, their manager, had come to prepare their first visit, which would be crucial for the band's future: "*The Beatles have broken every record imaginable in the entertainment world in England. They are the most adored and idolised boys in the country*," he declared at his press conference in New York in November 1963, before adding his own explanation for the burgeoning phenomenon: "*They have tremendous style, and a great effervescence, which communicates itself in an extraordinary way. Their beat is something like Rock'n'Roll but different from it. They are quite different from the big English rock'n'rollers in that they are not phony. They have none of that mean hardness about them. They are genuine. They have life, humour, and strange, handsome looks.*" In so many words, Epstein had managed to seduce the key media in the USA and, even if some American magazines immediately considered that they looked "*like shaggy Peter Pan with their mushroom haircuts*" (*Time magazine*, Nov. 15, 1963), or like "*sheep-dog bangs*" (*Newsweek*, Nov. 18, 1963), the king of American television had decided to book them for the following month.

On February 9, 1964, their "Ed Sullivan Show" appearance broke all its audience records (73 million viewers) and the United States recorded its lowest rate of burglaries that night. Consecrated by television in Great Britain, they were now consecrated by television in the United States. A few days earlier, "I Wanna Hold Your Hand" had topped

the American charts, an extremely rare event for an English group, and on April 12, 1964, The Beatles even snatched the top five places of the American charts, a record still unmatched today!

The Beatles on their first Ed Sullivan show, 1964

After Sweden and France, the 1964 tour swept the world and Beatlemania spread unvaryingly wherever the group was playing: in Denmark, Holland, Hong Kong, Australia and New Zealand, all the teenagers wanted to dress or talk like them, and Beatles wigs were all the rage. To find a safe haven in the eye of the hurricane, the four musicians then more or less consciously built a constant and solid carapace around themselves with their humour: *"We never believed in Beatlemania, never took the whole thing that seriously, I suppose. That way, we managed to stay sane."*(Paul McCartney, *Anthology*, 1995).

The next three years followed the same pattern, breaking new records with every tour: the apotheosis was reached when The Beatles invented stadium concerts, starting with the legendary Shea Stadium in New York on August 15, 1965. After landing in a helicopter on the lawn of the American Mecca of baseball where over 50,000 teenagers were screaming for them, their music was once again inaudible. With its 100-watt Vox amplifiers – made especially for the occasion – the sound system was utterly ineffective, and the musicians soon grew dissatisfied: *"It sounded pretty crummy on stage. So what we did with it (in the American tour at least) was get to the point where it was particularly bad, and then we'd do our 'Elvis legs' and wave to the crowd, and they'd all scream and it would cover that."* (George Harrison, *Anthology*, 1995).

Needless to say, even at the height of their fame, The Beatles did not garner only admiration: *"My dear girl, there are some things that just aren't done, such as drinking Dom Pérignon '53 above the temperature of 38 degrees Fahrenheit. That's just as bad as listening to The Beatles without earmuffs!"*, proclaimed James Bond in the 1964 movie *Goldfinger*. Today, one can still find traces of this visceral aversion here and there – although quite rarely in Great Britain or the United States – in songs (*"All that phoney Beatlemania has bitten the dust"*, The Clash, *London Calling*, 1979), in books (*Living Life Without Loving The Beatles: A Survivor's Guide*, Gary Hall, 2006) or on websites (*www.suckmybeatles.com*).

But John, Paul, George and Ringo themselves were the first to become weary of this lifestyle, spending most of their time barricaded in hotel rooms. Harrison, in particular, hated this confinement and was the first to find refuge in transcendental meditation. It was also he who pushed the group towards a radical decision after the summer of 1966.

The world tour had been particularly trying following a minor diplomatic incident in the Philippines when the band refused to attend an event organised by the President's wife, Imelda Marcos. This was followed one month later by the US media reaction to Lennon's controversial statements (*"we are more popular than Jesus"*): after playing one last time in San Francisco on August 28, 1966, The Beatles decided to stop touring and to devote their professional lives to studio work. Beatlemania declined almost immediately, leaving the world with only one question: why them?

The main factors lie, of course, in their music, a mix of energetic and cheerful Pop-Rock, as well as in their pertinent and impertinent humour. But other external elements can also be included in the equation: the search for a form of "soft rebellion" on the part of baby boomers, especially among girls, or the need to escape from a social, cultural and political environment that was still gloomy in the early 1960s. Ringo would later explain: "*I feel The Beatles were doing what they wanted to do, and a lot of it was that youthfulness of trying to change ideas. I think it allowed people to do things they wouldn't have done if we hadn't been out there.*" (*Anthology*, 1995).

As many journalists have already pointed out, The Beatles may simply have been the right band in the right place at the right time, always slightly ahead but never too far.

Are all Beatles movies rubbish?

An essentially feminine phenomenon, from which boys were never totally absent, the hysteria surrounding John, Paul, George and Ringo amused them, and was immediately the subject of a black and white movie in 1964. Originally entitled *Beatlemania*, the script for *A Hard Day's Night* was written by Alun Owen as he followed The Beatles on their travels in November 1963 to draw inspiration from their humour. An undeniable commercial success, it was also very well-received by many critics for its original and somewhat irreverent tone, the band being sometimes compared with Mack Sennett and the Marx Brothers!

In 1965, they followed this up with a colour movie: *Help!* was an insignificant amusement rooted in British nonsense, and was also a success in Great Britain, but ventured dangerously down the fan-comedy slope, which had seen the rise and demise of Elvis. The Beatles would not renew the experience and chose instead to direct their own psychedelic colour film, unfortunately broadcast in black and white on the BBC on December 26, 1967 ("Magical Mystery Tour"). The project was a total fiasco and the first real artistic setback for the band, who learned at their expense that you cannot improvise yourself as a director or as a scriptwriter.

In 1968, and after an initially tentative response to an animated film project, The Beatles eventually provided a few songs and participated in the final scene of *Yellow Submarine*, also rooted in the late sixties' psychedelic mood, which today appears as one of the sources of inspiration for the Monty Python TV shows and movies (some of which were produced by George Harrison, such as *Life of Brian* in 1979).

Still under a 1963 contract with United Artists which required their participation in a third movie, the group then came up with the idea of making a documentary about their rehearsals: in January 1969, they made the mistake of rehearsing in an unknown studio, surrounded by strangers who scrutinized and recorded each of their actions. The result, released in May 1970, as the movie *Let It Be* was at times pathetic and certainly showed the cracks and misunderstandings in the band rather than the friendship and the happiness: *"even the biggest Beatle fan couldn't have sat through those six weeks of misery. It was the most miserable session on earth."* (John Lennon, 1980).

Fans waited for decades for the re-release of the movie, which has now been re-edited by Peter Jackson (of *Lord of the Rings* fame) and given the new name *The Beatles: Get Back*. With a completely different and friendlier outlook on this period, it is set to be released in 2021.

04 – "The lyrics of the songs are often bland or weak."

> "Love, love me do, you know I love you
> I'll always be true, so please ..."
> Lennon / McCartney, 1962

In the distant time of the early sixties – the real prehistory of English Pop-Rock music – words and music were not treated as equals, far from it. Being a musician was what mattered. Writing texts was clearly secondary, and the lyrics only had to follow the rhythm of the music, a parameter greatly facilitated by the nature of the language: English poetry works by the number of *stressed* syllables in a given line, not by the total number of syllables, as does poetry in French for example.

The first song on The Beatles' debut album "I Saw Her Standing There" is an excellent example of this rhythmic efficiency, while also using a language perfectly adapted to the teenagers of the time:

She was just seventeen, you know what I mean

Up until their third album (*A Hard Day's Night*, July 1964), the words of The Beatles were undeniably insignificant for the most part. And it was probably no coincidence that obvious changes appeared after their first meeting with Bob Dylan in August 1964: a very slight effervescence could be felt almost immediately in the song "I'm a Loser" by John Lennon on the following album (*Beatles for Sale*, December 1964):

Bob Dylan, 1963

34

Although I laugh and I act like a clown
Beneath this mask I'm wearing a frown...

The poetry of Lennon and McCartney became more tangible from 1965, with some lyrics moving away from the innocent conventions of the 'boy-loves-girl' type. Some of their texts can even be legitimately considered as complete works in their own right, expressing deep personal feelings, such as Lennon's unambiguous call for "Help!" in 1965:

My life has changed in oh! so many ways
My independence seems to vanish in the haze

And again in 1965 on "Rubber Soul", with Lennon's alter ego, "Nowhere Man":

Sitting in his nowhere land
Making all his nowhere plans for nobody
Isn't he a bit like you and me?

But the real turning point came with their sixth British album in 1966, *Revolver*. Its opening track "Taxman", was George Harrison's sarcastic declaration of war on the UK taxation system:

If you drive a car, I'll tax the street,
If you try to sit, I'll tax your seat
If you get too cold, I'll tax the heat
If you take a walk, I'll tax your feet...

Followed by McCartney's imaginary "Eleanor Rigby", who:

picks up the rice in a church
Where a wedding has been...
All the lonely people, where do they all come from?

And the final track, "Tomorrow Never Knows" by Lennon, summed up the spirit of the times with its experimental music and lyrics:

Turn off your mind relax and float down-stream,
But listen to the colour of your dreams...

The 1967 song "Lucy In The Sky With Diamonds" is particularly representative of John Lennon's psychedelic period. Although he consistently claimed to have been inspired by a drawing by his 4 year-old son Julian – and not by the hallucinogenic drug represented in the three initials of the song – very few doubts remain about the origin of the surrealist evocations:

Picture yourself in a boat on a river,
With tangerine trees and marmalade skies,
Somebody calls you and you answer quite slowly
A girl with kaleidoscope eyes.

One should also remember, however, that John was a great admirer of Lewis Carroll, and that his lyrics were always imbued with a great deal of imaginary fantasy, as in "Julia" (1968), written in memory of his mother:

Julia, seashell eyes, windy smiles, calls me
Julia, sleeping sand, silent cloud, touch me

or as in "Across The Universe" (1969):
Words are flowing out like endless rain
Into a paper cup.
Thoughts meander like a restless wind
Inside a letterbox

The latter, although apparently characteristic of a chaotic text written under the influence, is in fact carefully structured and displays great poetic rigour. It was also one of his favourites.

The lyrics to "I Am The Walrus" (1967) are often cited as an example of pure Lennon-esque nonsense, sometimes bordering on the grotesque:

I am he as you are he as you are me
And we are all together
See how they run like pigs from a gun see how they fly,
I'm crying

Sitting on a corn flake waiting for the van to come
Corporation T-shirt, stupid bloody Tuesday,
man you've been a naughty boy,
You let your face grow long
I am the egg man, they are the egg men,
I am the walrus, Goo goo g'joob

But here again, John's objective becomes a lot clearer when we know that, having heard that his songs were now being studied at school, he had set out to explore the boundaries of surrealism, and possibly compose a meaningless text for the single purpose of mystifying everyone: "*The way it's written, everybody presumes that means something. I mean, even I did. We all just presumed that because I said 'I am the Walrus' that it must mean 'I am God' or something. It's just poetry, but it became symbolic of me.*" (J. Lennon, 1970).

Paul McCartney had a very different approach to writing and preferred the subtle evocation of characters and feelings. This was most often expressed in a pessimistic way, reaching its highest literary intensity in his darker texts, like "Yesterday" (1965):
Suddenly, I'm not half the man I used to be
There's a shadow hanging over me ...
Why she had to go? I don't know, she wouldn't say...

or "The Long And Winding Road" (1969):
The long and winding road that leads to your door
Will never disappear, I've seen that road before ...

And one of his most beautiful texts remains his half-word evocation of the struggle of black American women in "Blackbird" (1968):
Blackbird singing in the dead of night,
Take these broken wings and learn to fly,

All your life, you were only waiting for this moment to arise.

In 2001, a selection of McCartney's best lyrics and poems of the period 1965-1999 was published under the title *Blackbird Singing, the poetry of Paul McCartney*.

George Harrison, finally, was primarily inspired by his personal reflections on society and developed a somewhat corrosive style of writing, as in this mordant vision of the British upper-class:
Everywhere there's lots of piggies living piggy lives
You can see them out for dinner with their piggy wives
Clutching forks and knives to eat their bacon...
("Piggies", 1968)

As time went by, he also developed a penchant for mystical lyrics, as in "Within You, Without You" in 1967:
We were talking about the space around us,
And people who hide behind a wall of illusion ...

or in "The Inner Light", 1968 :
Without getting out of my door,
I can know all things on earth,
The farther one travels, the less one knows...

And of course, one should also pay special attention – among George's 22 tracks recorded with the group – to one of the most admirable love songs ever written, which Frank Sinatra once described comically as his "favourite Lennon & McCartney song"!:
Somewhere in her smile she knows
That I don't need no other lover
I don't want to leave her now
You know I believe and how
("Something", 1969)

These short examples, among many others, certainly do not make McCartney, Lennon and Harrison role models among the poets of the 20th century. Still, they clearly demonstrate their ability to write finely crafted texts whose significance reaches far beyond the innocence, futility and misogyny of their early sixties creations.

05 - "There was a fifth Beatle."

> *"Brian's judgment was extremely fair. He never misguided us. If there ever was a fifth Beatle, it was Brian."*
> Paul McCartney, 1997

It would be difficult to ignore that there were four members in the *Fab Four*. And it would not have occurred to anyone at the time that one of them could be replaced, unlike what has happened several times with the Rolling Stones over the decades. The coveted title of "Fifth Beatle" however, is one of the most widespread accolades given to some of their direct entourage, most often awarded by the media. The expression was probably first used by American DJ Murray The K for his own benefit, while promoting the group's arrival in the USA in February 1964. But around John, Paul, George and Ringo were countless other unsung heroes, far more deserving of the title.

Musicians who can boast of having performed under The Beatles name form a very closed circle, and Stuart Sutcliffe can arguably be considered as the most eminent among them. Not that his musical talents were immense, far from it, but his very close friendship with John Lennon, and later his clothing choices and his hairstyle, had a decisive influence on the image of the group. A particularly gifted abstract painter, and John Lennon's best friend, Stu Sutcliffe became The Beatles bassist in 1960 simply by purchasing his first ever instrument thanks to the sale of one of his own paintings. He then accompanied them during their musical stays in Hamburg in 1960 and 1961, where he eventually decided to stay in order to devote himself entirely to painting, but sadly died on April 10, 1962 of a cerebral haemorrhage. His memory remained long intact in the minds of The Beatles, and his effigy was later used for the cover of the *Sergeant Pepper's* album in 1967, built around the concept of 'people who mattered' for the band.

The same cannot be said of the unfortunate Peter Best, however, who was the first real Beatles' drummer: recruited on August 12, 1960 on the eve of their departure for their first contract in Hamburg, he was considered musically inadequate by producer George Martin during their very first recording session on June 6, 1962 ("Love Me Do"): he was quickly replaced by Ringo Starr, whose wit and humour appealed much more to John, Paul and George. This has earned Pete Best the adverse nickname of "unluckiest musician in the world".

The Beatles producer himself, George Martin, an excellent musician and arranger, is rightly considered as a determining component of the group's musical evolution from 1962 onwards. Classically trained, director of the Parlophone label at the age of 29, he had distinguished himself within the London EMI studios at Abbey Road for his productions in the field of comedy, in particular with Peter Sellers. At 36, and looking for new adventures in the field of Pop-Rock music, he immediately understood the value and significance of a band who could write their own songs.

The personalities of The Beatles were probably at least as important as their musical qualities when they first met: as legend would have it, when he had finished explaining how recording sessions worked and inquired if they had any questions or remarks, George Harrison wryly replied with the confidence of a 19 year-old man: "*Well, I don't like your tie for a start*". The ice was broken and the most prolific musical collaboration of the 1960s could begin.

With the exception of the album *Let It Be* (produced by Phil Spector and released in 1970) as well as the song "She's Leaving Home" (1967), George Martin produced all the group's compositions, in a constant atmosphere of openness and total honesty, as John Lennon noted in 1964: "(He) *can read music, so sometimes he'll say 'That note's just... it doesn't work, you know. You can't have it.' (...) And sometimes he's right, sometimes he's wrong, you know. But it usually all works out in the end.*"

More of an arranger than a technician or a sound engineer, his contributions quickly went from the simple addition of keyboards (in 1963 on "Misery" and "You Really Got A Hold On Me", or in 1965 on "In My Life") to more complex arrangements, an integral part of The Beatles' sound ("Yesterday" in 1965, "Eleanor Rigby" in 1966). His creativity and inventiveness, sometimes pushed to their limits by requests bordering on the impossible – juxtaposing two different versions of "Strawberry Fields Forever" in 1967, for instance – earned him the privilege to be inducted into the Rock and Roll Hall of Fame in 1999 and to be knighted by the Queen in 1996.

Of course, many other members of the inner circle have sometimes been endowed with the title of "Fifth Beatle", such as Mal Evans, the ubiquitous friend and assistant of the band from their early years; Neil Aspinall, a friend of the early days and later director of their Apple company from 1968 to 2007; or Derek Taylor, a journalist and press officer ; or even Norman Smith and Geoff Emerick, two of the group's main sound engineers.

But the title of "Fifth Beatle" indisputably goes, as George Martin himself often pointed out, to their discreet and omnipresent manager, Brian Epstein. Born to a wealthy Jewish family in

Liverpool and a homosexual at a time when this preference was still regarded as a felony in English law, he dithered for a while between different careers (acting, *haute couture*, furniture stores...) before enthusiastically taking up the management of the recently created record section of the family store in 1958. It was ob-viously in this context that he heard about The Beatles, who frequently appeared on the front page of the local music magazine, *Mersey Beat*, in which his store regularly advertised.

Brian Epstein in 1965

Determined to become their manager after seeing them on stage in Liverpool's tiny Cavern club in November 1961, he tried unsuccessfully to have them signed by Columbia, Pye, Philips, Oriole, HMV and Decca. It took all his determination and his unshakeable faith in his 'boys' (he had proclaimed on several occasions that they would one day be "greater than Elvis") for Parlophone, a subsidiary of EMI, to finally decide to open their doors.

But his work was in no way restricted to this contract, nor to the success of what would become his Merseyside 'stable' (Gerry and the Peacemakers, Billy J. Kramer and the Dakotas, the Fourmost, Cilla Black and many others): a very discreet personality, he was also a born diplomat and managed to convince The Beatles to play in suits, not to smoke or drink on stage, and suggested that they bow at the end of each song. Above all, he had the intelligence to leave all creative latitude to his artists, unlike what Colonel Parker did with Elvis Presley, for example. So much so that Brian's autobiography, written in 1964, relates with a slight bitterness the scathing response of John Lennon when he dared make a comment during a recording session: "*You look after your percentages, Brian, and we'll take care of the music*". Decorated in 1965 as Members of the British Empire (MBE), Paul McCartney and George Harrison later exclaimed "*MBE stands for 'Mr. Brian Epstein !'*".

The death of their manager at the age of 32 from an accidental overdose of sleeping pills on August 27, 1967, marked the beginning of the end for the group which was left to their own device. They soon launched their own company (Apple Corps in 1968) and slowly but surely edged closer to their separation, formally announced in April 1970. Lennon would later declare about Brian's death: "*I knew that we were in trouble then. I didn't really have any misconceptions about our ability to do anything other than play music, and I was scared. I thought, 'We've had it now.'*"

Other names, sometimes famous, also appear in this long list because of their participation in such and such recording session: Eric Clapton, for his guitar solo on "While My Guitar Gently Weeps" in 1968; The Rolling Stones' Brian Jones for his saxophone solo on "You Know My Name (Look Up The Number)" in 1967; Billy Preston for his keyboard contribution during the *Let It Be* sessions in 1969; Phil Spector for his production work on the album of the same name, and many more.

But one simple question remains at the end of this long list of names,: where does this obsession with "fifth Beatles" come from, even after more than 50 years since the band's breakup? After all, no one has ever tried to find a "fourth musketeer" or Vivaldi's "fifth season", have they?

06 - "The Beatles music was plain, simplistic pop."

> "Musically they are a near disaster, guitars and drums slamming out a merciless beat that does away with secondary rhythms, harmony and melody. Their lyrics (punctuated by nutty shouts of "yeah, yeah, yeah") are a catastrophe, a preposterous farrago of Valentine-card romantic sentiments. The odds are they will fade away, as most adults confidently predict."
>
> *Newsweek*, Feb. 24, 1964

> "The Beatles were one-of-a-kind and a blessing to the music world, each and every one of them."
>
> James Brown, in *Memories of John Lennon*, by Yoko Ono, 2005

Beatles specialists tend to consider the musical career of the group in three periods: the initial cycle, from 1962 to 1965, ended with their first attempt to break open the Pop-Rock cast ("Yesterday", on the album *Help!* in August 1965), an experiment that was soon converted into the exploratory album *Rubber Soul* in December of the same year. Then came the experimental phase, from 1966 to 1967, which represents their creative peak, with *Revolver* (August 1966) and of course *Sergeant Pepper's...* (June 1967), followed by *Magical Mystery Tour* (1967). The final period began with the so-called 'White' album (November 1968), followed by *Abbey Road* (September 1969) and finally *Let It Be* (recorded in January 1969 but only released in May 1970).

Despite these evolutions, one of the constant hallmarks of The Beatles' music was that apparent melodic simplicity, too often equated with musical deficiency: but it would be very wrong to believe that the initial period of the group's career contains only simplistic catchy melodies devoid of any musical interest. The illustrious music critic for the British daily newspaper The Times, William Mann – although not quite familiar with the Rock'n'Roll paradigm – perceived as early as November 1963 the genuine subversion behind the apparent plainness: "*one gets the impression that they think simultaneously of harmony and melody, so firmly are the major tonic sevenths and ninths built into their tunes, and the flat submediant key switches, so natural is the Aeolian cadence at the end of "Not a second time" (the chord progression which ends Mahler's Song of the Earth)*". In 1980, when asked by a journalist about those Aeolian cadences, John Lennon admitted with amusement that, like the vast majority of Rock and Pop musicians: "*To this day I don't have any idea what they are. They sound like exotic birds* (*Playboy* interview).

The Beatles had no formal musical training whatsoever, and Paul explained as late as 2000: "*To this day I have never learnt to write or read music; I have a vague suspicion now that it would change how I'd do things*". As has often been said, their songs give the impression of being composed out of established standards, or even haphazardly. But this ignorance of music theory was soon transformed into musical instinct as illustrated by a quick analysis of the 1964 hit "A Hard Day's Night", the result of a real cooperation between John and Paul: the chord progression (G / C / F / D / Bbm / Em) already demonstrates the use of interesting harmonic innovations for Pop-Rock music (including a bridge in Bb minor), as well as some original melodic dissonances (including the D note sung on a C chord for "*...day's...*"). But more than anything, it was the astonishing opening chord that grabbed the attention: book chapters have been written solely about the effect of surprise and expectation produced by this introductory sequence. [For the inquisitive readers, and according to the latest analyses, it seems George played an F add9 on the guitar, based on the notes G-C-A-F, augmented by an A played by Paul on the bass, as well as a D-F-G-C-D chord on the piano and a snare drum hit].

Three years later, the opening bars of the song "I Am The Walrus" (1967) offer another fascinating example of this contrast between complexity and simplicity, illustrated by a deliberately repetitive vocal line, as explained by John: "*I had this idea of doing a song that was a police siren, (…) 'I-am-he-as-you-are-he-a…', [but] you couldn't really sing the police siren*"(*Rolling Stone* , Nov. 1968). The contrast with the complexity of the first measures on the keyboard is however perfectly mastered: from four simple guitar chords for "I Saw Her Standing There" in 1963, we move up to 16 chords on the keyboard, eight of them in the first 20 seconds. This is also something that many young musicians soon discover when they try to cover Beatles songs: yes indeed, they are very far from being as simple as they sound!

As composers, no serious analyst today considers the music of The Beatles to be naive formatted pop, quite the contrary actually. And countless examples can be given here, from the constant oscillation between major and minor keys in "And I Love her" (1964) to the seven key modulations in "Penny Lane" augmented by a baroque trumpet (1966); from guitar arpeggios on "Blackbird" (1968) to the piano bassline of "Lady Madonna" (1968) through the odd time signatures hidden in "We can Work it Out" (1965) and "Here Comes the Sun" (1969), or the Dorian and Mixolydian modes in "Eleanor Rigby" (1966) or "Dear Prudence" (1968).

Objective listeners will of course concede some weaknesses in the group's vast catalogue ("Little Child", "Maxwell's Silver Hammer",…), but these rare moments when The Beatles reached their artistic limits still remained well above the general level of Rock musicians and composers of the time.

Technically, The Beatles never tried to compete with guitarists like Jimi Hendrix or drummers like Keith Moon, but again it would be very wrong to regard them as poor musicians: it was precisely in this artistic sobriety that the group developed its style and creativity, focusing only on the interaction between sounds in order to create a homogenous result, assisted and pushed on by their producer George Martin, who declared in 1998: "*They were far more than the sum of the parts, there was a fusion of the four that made them shine even more. It was almost like a nuclear explosion, actually*".

Few singers, however, can compete with the inventiveness and musical precision of the three voices of John, Paul or George, weaving complex harmonies with disconcerting ease, from "She Loves You" (1963) to "Because" (1969), and shifting effortlessly from the wildest songs ("Twist and Shout", "I'm Down") to the most moving ballads ("Yesterday", "Julia", "Something").

John, Paul, George, 1968

The second hallmark of the group, and ultimately the most important, was the idea that nothing is impossible: all it takes is a little time or imagination. Who else, for example, would have dared to release a song over seven minutes long on the A-side of a single, half of which was spent repeating "na-na-na..." ("Hey Jude", 1968)?

This is why wondering whether The Beatles played Pop or Rock music – as is so often heard – is quite useless: they played both, and much more besides, depending on their moods and ideas. If, in

1963, popular music was defined by watertight categories ranked in entirely different charts, the 'White' album alone (in 1968) displayed productions of Pop, Rock, Hard-Rock, Folk, Blues, Country, Reggae, avant-garde and symphonic influences, all of which rendered this artificial division completely obsolete by 1970.

07 - "Sgt Pepper's *is the best Beatles album.*"

> *"It was a peak. Paul and I were definitely working together."*
> John Lennon, *Rolling Stone* interview, 1970.

Released on June 1st 1967 after months of questions and doubts on the part of the British media regarding the band's future, *Sgt Pepper's Lonely Hearts Club Band* is the album of all superlatives, immediately considered by the general public and critics as *"a decisive moment in the history of Western civilization"* as music critic Kenneth Tynan wrote in The Times at the time of its release.

The Beatles' 8th album, which entered the British charts one week before its official release (!), remained at the top for almost six months (but only three and a half months in the USA) and received four Grammy Awards in 1968. It has since sold almost 40 million copies in 50 years and is regularly ranked the No. 1 record of all time, most famously in "The 500 Greatest Albums of All Time", a 2003 special issue of the American magazine *Rolling Stone*.

On August 29, 1966, The Beatles gave in San Francisco what would remain as their final real concert. Exhausted by years of constant recording and non-stop touring (7 albums and approximately 1400 concerts in 3 years!), They decided to devote themselves solely to studio work (a decision also made by classical pianist Glenn Gould in 1964). A turning point for The Beatles, it was an even more important turning point for the world of music, in particular with the clear supremacy of recording over live concerts, which would last for more than thirty years, until the arrival of mp3 recordings.

"We were fed up with being The Beatles," McCartney told his biographer in 1997: And so he came up with the idea of creating a fictitious band, a façade to hide behind, the fanfare of a lonely hearts club, a vague concept that would serve as the basis for the album's creation: *"It liberated you - you could do anything when you got to the mike or on your guitar, because it wasn't you"*, as he also explained in the *Anthology* documentary (1995).

Between November 1966 and April 1967, the band recorded more than 15 songs in 700 hours at Abbey Road Studios in north-west London: 13 of them would appear on the album, while two others (McCartney's "Penny Lane" and Lennon's "Strawberry Fields Forever") were to be released as a single in February, but not included on the album. Their producer George Martin would later concede that this separation was *"a terrible mistake"*.

It has often been remarked that England is represented on this album as an eternal, slightly outdated country. But it is just as ready to shift into another era: from the clarinets in "When I'm Sixty-Four" to the generational conflict in "She's Leaving Home", from the music hall atmosphere of "With a Little Help from my Friends" to a stimulating everyday life in "A Day in the Life", Good Old England is ready to change gear.

But above all, the brand new psychedelic energy of the album prefigures what 1967 and its "Summer of Love" would be remembered as: "Lucy in the Sky with Diamonds", probably inspired to John by a drawing by his son Julian, described the surreal gallery of a daydreamer, while "Being for the Benefit of Mr Kite" was inspired by an 1843 circus poster, and "Within You, Without You" offered a long and serious meditative break of oriental inspiration – soon followed by a burst of self-mocking laughter.

On a technical level, innovations and experiments also far surpassed anything that had been done so far. Equipped only with a 4-track tape recorder – a far cry from today's computers and their almost infinite number of tracks – The Beatles and their collaborators Geoff Emerick and George Martin competed in ingenuity to find new sounds and new ideas, pushing the equipment to its limits and exploring all its possibilities.

Among the countless artistic innovations that have since become commonplace in studios and home-studios are some incredible sound collages in "Being for the Benefit of Mr Kite", a drum kit sound of rare intensity in "Strawberry Fields Forever", a formidable symphonic crescendo in "A Day in the Life", ultra high frequencies in the final seconds of the vinyl groove, and countless other discreet sonic nuggets to discover for yourself.

If you add to this list of novelties the lyrics of the songs, printed for the first time on the cover of a Rock album – which has itself remained famous for its complexity and grandiose scale – you might begin to understand why this album is undoubtedly one of the first masterpieces of Rock music, an undisputed symbol of the psychedelic period.

Since nobody's perfect, however, The Beatles once again forgot to disclose the names of the countless musicians who participated in its creation, from the horn quartet on "Sgt Pepper's..." to the brass section on "Good Morning, Good Morning", from Indian musicians on "Within You, Without You" to the harpist on "She's Leaving Home", and so on. Those were the days...

Beatles specialists, and more generally connoisseurs of Rock music, know that the so-called "Beatles revolution" did not begin in 1967, but more likely with the two previous albums, in 1965 and 1966. After 5 solid Pop-Rock albums between 1963 and mid-1965 (including the first one recorded in a single day!), change came inconspicuously with *Rubber Soul* (1965), which features one of the very first uses of the Indian sitar in pop music ("Norwegian Wood"), as well as tentative philosophical reflections ("Nowhere Man", "Girl") or a *naïve* approach to the precepts of Peace and Love ("The Word").

One year before *Sergeant Pepper's*, the movement accelerated with their 7th album, *Revolver*, where allusions to drugs became a little bit more obvious ("She Said, She Said" or "I'm Only Sleeping"). The melodies were also more elaborate and the arrangements more sophisticated ("Eleanor Rigby", "For No One"). But it is above all the final track, "Tomorrow Never Knows", which remains to this day an object of admiration for millions of musicians: based on a single C chord, the song floats for three minutes above a solid drumbeat, a hovering collage of multiple ingredients, often imitated and rarely equalled: inverted loops of various instruments, lyrics of mystical inspiration, innovative recording techniques, especially on drums and voices, etc. The result is a work of art that is still regarded today as a turning point in recording. Listening to this track, recorded as early as April 1966, anyone can understand why The Beatles were tired of still playing songs like "I Feel Fine" or "I Wanna Be Your Man" that summer, in front of an audience that did not even listen to them...

The immediate sequel to *Sgt Pepper's...* was much less glorious. Their first project after the death of their manager Brian Epstein in August 1967, the psychedelic-inspired film entitled "Magical Mystery Tour", was broadcast in black and white on British television on 26 December 1967. It was very severely judged by critics and audiences alike and very few songs were praised, with the notable exception of the outstanding "I Am the Walrus", whose false simplicity was again one of the main trademarks of the group.

Collectively, the decline continued between April and October 1968 with the recording sessions for what was to become the double album "The Beatles" (quickly nicknamed the 'White' album). Released in November of the same year, it was mostly written in India during their initiation to transcendental meditation from February to April 1968. This first opus published under their new Apple label was imbued with great simplicity, spontaneity and exuberance and, in a way, was the complete opposite of *Sgt Pepper's*.

In particular, the album uncovered the rare sensitivity of John Lennon with songs like "Julia" (dedicated to his mother), "Dear Prudence" or "Cry, Baby, Cry", all composed on the acoustic guitar. The record also gave pride of place to raging Blues or Rock tracks, whether by Lennon ("Yer Blues", "I'm So Tired", "Revolution 1", "Everybody's Got

Something To Hide..."), or by McCartney ("Back in the USSR", "Birthday", "Helter Skelter", "Why Don't We Do It In the Road?"). Although the album as a whole might sound like a motley crew of unrelated tracks, revealing the underlying quarrels between the four members during its genesis, it allowed The Beatles to push their own musical boundaries once again, as well as those of their fans. Like "Revolution 9", an avant-garde mix of sounds and sound effects that left no one indifferent, this ninth album remains more of a collage of individualities than a true collective undertaking.

Yellow Submarine, the album accompanying the eponymous animated feature in 1969, is also strikingly heterogeneous, a compilation of different songs put together for good measure rather than a *bona fide* album. Even more disappointing for the fans, the second side only consisted of the classical pieces that illustrated the film, composed by their producer George Martin.

The fragmentation of The Beatles' identity continued in 1969 with *Get Back*, a project imagined by McCartney as a return to their roots and filmed for posterity. This would soon be interpreted as a public disintegration of the group. A few excerpts from the January 1969 sessions, cleverly remixed a year later by Phil Spector (much to McCartney's despair), constitute the raw material for *Let It Be*, The Beatles' twelfth album, released in May 1970.

Although slightly veiled by Spector's overproduction, one can nevertheless find some traits of genius and musical cohesion in Lennon's "Don't Let Me Down", Harrison's "I Me Mine", or McCartney's "Get Back" and "Let It Be". Ultimately, McCartney would have to wait for over 30 years to see his dream come true: in 2003, the same album was released without Phil Spector's heavy symphonic production, under the new title of *Let It Be… Naked*.

Undermined by internal quarrels, but lucid about the future of the group, the four members met again in the summer of 1969, determined to make a success of their next album. George Martin, their regular producer, was once again part of their project and remembers a joyous period, "probably because everyone knew it would be their last album" (1995).

Over 50 years after its recording, "Abbey Road" – the eleventh album of the band since it was released before "Let It Be" – remains a monument of extraordinary clarity and inventiveness: from a masterful funky opening by Lennon wrapped around McCartney's bass ("Come Together") to the final triple guitar solo by Lennon, Harrison and McCartney in "The End", from the acrobatic vocal harmonies of "Because" to Harrison's two masterpieces ("Something" and "Here Comes the Sun"), the album spent more than 4 months at the top of the English charts and remains to this day the band's second best selling opus (after the 'White' album) with over 30 million copies sold.

One can therefore legitimately challenge *Sergeant Pepper's…* the title of "best Beatles album", since no one will ever agree on the artistic criteria to be taken into account. What remains is an album (and more precisely a vinyl LP in its original format) released on June 1st 1967, which left an indelible imprint on its time like no other before or since, with its multifaceted and ground-breaking originality.

08 – "John was the rebellious avant-gardist, Paul the charming businessman."

John: *"we want to set up a system whereby people who just want to make a film about … anything, don't have to go on their knees in somebody's office. Probably yours."*

Paul: *"We're in the happy position of not really needing any more money. So for the first time, the bosses aren't in it for profit."*

Apple press conference, New York, 11 May 1968.

From the very first moments of The Beatles' fame in 1963, the British and American media decided to label its four members: while George was *"the quiet Beatle"* and Ringo *"the funny Beatle"*, McCartney, regarded as the author of the most romantic songs, was immediately considered *"the cute Beatle"*, always ready to smile for cameras and answer questions from journalists, especially women. In early 1964, Lennon published a rather successful collection of humorous short stories (*In His Own Write*), followed by a second one in 1965 (*A Spaniard In The Works*), and was soon called *"the intellectual Beatle"*. His introspective lyrics ("In My Life", 1965, or "Nowhere Man", 1966) reinforced this perception in the eyes of the general public.

Later, while Paul and Ringo continued to accept their stardom and play with it – at least with the media – John and George chose to shed that cumbersome image and to allow themselves greater freedom of expression. George Harrison explained in 1995: *"The Beatles exist apart from my Self. I am not really 'Beatle George'. 'Beatle George' is like a suit or shirt that I once wore on occasion and until the end of my life people may see that shirt and mistake it for me."* (*Newsweek*, Oct 22 1995).

During his brief period of political commitment (1969-1972), John's most incisive songs and experiments definitively placed him among the leading intellectual artists of the time: visually with his famous round glasses and long hair of course, but most notably with songs like "Revolution" and "Revolution 9" on the 'White' album in 1968, as well as with his activism for the pacifist cause from 1969 onwards.

But several factors should nuance this vision, and first and foremost some of McCartney's songs: While not all of his social commentaries are as vivid as Lennon's, some of Paul's lyrics clearly carry within them a critical analysis of this period, be it about poverty ("Eleanor Rigby", 1966 or "Lady Madonna", 1968), intolerance ("The Fool On The Hill", 1967), or racism ("Blackbird", 1968 as well as the original version of "Get Back", 1969, prompted by a hate speech by far-right politician Enoch Powell).

John's positions have sometimes been considered *naïve* and irrational, as when he suddenly became passionate about transcendental meditation in 1967, or about politics from 1968 onwards ("Revolution"). But it was also John who wrote "All You Need Is Love" for a television programme broadcast live around the world in June 1967. And it was George – not John – who convinced the four members of the group to go to India and find peace of mind with a guru in February 1968: Ringo stayed 10 days, Paul one month, George and John two months, and all four of them regretted it at the time.

One aspect of the group's life that did not interest Lennon at all, however, was the management of their business, an interest that was more apparent in Harrison and McCartney. Paul, living in central London unlike the other three, was also very much in the *Swinging London* scene of the 1960s; concerts, plays, experiments, painting exhibitions, antique shops, new media, clothing: everything that was fashionable at the time was of interest to him, and the psychedelic film *Magical Mystery Tour* would never have seen the light of day without his input. After the death of their manager Brian Epstein in August 1967, it was also he who took charge of the future of their new company. As Neil Aspinall – a childhood friend and later director of Apple Corps – explained: *"It was Paul who found the name Apple, inspired by René Magritte (...). I know that Paul bought some of his paintings in 1966 or early 1967, I think that's where Paul found the name"*.

In fact, and contrary to what is generally believed, Paul was most in tune with the avant-garde milieu of the time and became interested in avant-garde electronic music as early as 1965, long before John; he even contacted the BBC's special effects department at the time to consider an innovative sound accompaniment on the song "Yesterday" (fortunately without following it up!). It was also Paul who first became interested in philosophy with intellectuals such as Bertrand Russell, whom he met in 1966 and who impressed him with his passion for pacifism; or in experimental compositions such as those of John Cage or Karlheinz Stockhausen, whose portrait he chose to have on the cover of *Sergeant Pepper's* (June 1967).

Finally, at Paul's instigation, a 14-minute experimental piece entitled "Carnival of Light" was recorded in January 1967 for broadcast at an underground event at the Roundhouse in London. Unfortunately, it is one of the extremely rare Beatles tracks that have never been released, not even on bootleg recordings.

Considering Paul as a determined businessman is also entirely justified, all the more so as he was the first – along with George – to hate being taken for a ride, particularly by unscrupulous businessmen in the show business world. But he was also the first avant-gardist of the band, something he has been trying to explain, mostly in vain, for over 50 years in his interviews, much to his chagrin. One will however concede that the term "charmer" also suits him perfectly.

As for John, his rebellious character was firmly established during the period 1966-1972. But it is slightly ironic that, to this day, this has remained the image permanently attached to his character, although he spent the last 5 years of his life in voluntary retirement, considering himself first and foremost as a househusband.

The 'Paul is dead' rumour

Born in the fertile imagination of some American students in Iowa in September 1969, rumour has it that Paul died in a car accident on Wednesday, November 9, 1966 at 5 a.m., and was immediately replaced by a perfect look-alike called William Shears Campbell.

The hoax was reported the following month by a DJ and picked up on by other students in Michigan, who by their own admission made up many of the clues that are still being repeated to this day. These imaginary clues, based mainly on the symbolism of the covers and recordings, then attracted the attention of the major American and international media.

The cover of the *Abbey Road* album, for example, is full of these "determining" elements: Paul is the only one walking barefoot, he is walking out of step with the others, he holds his cigarette in his right hand although he is left-handed, and the car number plate in the background reads "28IF", which supposedly meant "McCartney would have been 28 IF he hadn't died". Except that the number plate was really 281F... among other simple refutations of the so-called clues.

Many other alleged clues and macabre interpretations were offered at that time, which prompted *Life Magazine* to send two journalists to meet McCartney and his family. All the rumours were disproved in the November 7, 1969 issue: "*if the conclusion*

you reach is that I am dead, then you are wrong,
because I am very much alive, I am alive and
living in Scotland". The *soufflé* collapsed
almost immediately. Or almost, since the
advent of the internet somewhat revived the
rumour-mongering business in the late 90s,
and we still hear from time to time
seemingly serious people devoting lengthy
studies to this absurd story.

More seriously, the existence of this
rumour can be accounted for by several
valid elements: the public's need to elucidate
the group's meteoric evolution from 1966
onwards, the intuition that all was not going
well in The Beatles' universe, and the credit
given to the new alternative media, as
opposed to the established media, whether
in the 70s or today.

09 - "George and Ringo were not good musicians."

"You don't just dismiss George like that! There's a hell of a lot more to him than that! And Ringo. The truth of this kind of question depends on where you're looking... on the surface or below the surface."
Paul McCartney, *Playboy* interview, 1984

In the show business world, Ringo Starr is sometimes described as the luckiest musician ever, the drummer hired to replace Peter Best in August 1962, just a few weeks before the release of The Beatles' first single, "Love Me Do". And if you add to this John Lennon's quip according to which "*Ringo wasn't even the best drummer in The Beatles*" (since George and, more importantly, Paul were both extremely competent in this area), it soon becomes clear why his role may have seemed minimal to the general public.

But such an dismissive approach clearly overlooks his immense qualities as a musician, namely: absolute precision, remarkable moderation and total efficiency. "*On only a handful of occasions during all of the several hundred session tapes and thousand of recording hours can Ringo be heard to have made a mistake or wavered in his beat. His work was remarkably consistent — and excellent — from 1962 right through to 1970,*" explained Mark Lewisohn, one of the group's main specialists (*The Beatles Recording Sessions*, 1988).

The difference between Ringo's creativity and that of other good drummers can easily be measured by listening to three Beatles tracks: "Back In The USSR", "Dear Prudence" and "The Ballad of John & Yoko" on which, for various reasons, McCartney played both bass and drums. Paul's technique is faultless and the drumming excellent, but it is far from the monumental inventiveness found in "Strawberry Fields Forever", "A Day In The Life" or "Come Together", for example. And in this respect, Ringo has often explained that his resourceful technique came from his three partners' constant demands: *"I was lucky enough to be surrounded by three frustrated drummers and each of them thought I was an octopus. They forgot I only had two hands and two feet."* (Ringo Star, *Musician Magazine*, 1991).

Being left-handed, but playing as a right-handed drummer (on his famous Ludwig Super Classic kit), he admitted himself that he wasn't an outstanding technician, preferring to give his instincts free rein to better serve the melody, without ever trying to put himself in the limelight: the epitome of this self-effacing drumming style can be found on John's song "In My Life" where Ringo uses one of the simplest drumbeats ever, and without any doubt the most effective for this particular song. After 7 years in the band, it took a lot of persuasion from the other members of the band in 1969 to finally get him to record a drum solo on the *Abbey Road* album, the only one in the band's career.

Apart from his identifiable style, which is based on a prominent but discreet use of toms and hi-hat cymbals, Ringo Starr also had a tendency to tune his drumheads very low, thus setting him significantly apart from the Jazz style of drumming most common in the 50s and early 60s. He is also credited with widely popularizing the symmetrical holding of sticks in the Rock style (rather than the asymmetrical manner of former military and Jazz band drummers), as well as the use of a raised dais on concert stages to enhance the visibility of the drummer.

As American drummer Kenny Aronoff noted in 1987: "*Lennon took to abstract lyrics and his acid rock guitar style, McCartney broadened and refined his compositional technique, and Harrison developed a passion for real Indian music and Indian instruments. Meanwhile, Ringo had the merit of adapting to everyone's style*".

There's however much more to Ringo's contribution than the technical aspects: his character and sense of humour also played a great part in his popularity and that of The Beatles. Archive footage of press conferences show, for example, alongside a bitter-sweet John and a diplomatic Paul, a happy-go-lucky Ringo answering journalists in a very tongue-in-cheek manner, often catching them off guard with pure British spontaneity and nonsense ("*What do you think of Beethoven?*" "*I love him, especially his poems*" New York, 7 February 1964). Ringo was also responsible for such unlikely expressions as "A Hard Day's Night", "Eight Days A Week" and "Tomorrow Never Knows", which immediately became musical inspirations for Lennon and McCartney.

Finally, what would The Beatles' repertoire be without Ringo's baritone voice, present on every album, from songs like "Yellow Submarine" to "With A Little Help From My Friends" or "Good Night", all written specifically for him? And remember, he actually did compose two very honourable tracks in 1968 and 1969, "Don't Pass Me By" and "Octopus's Garden" – although George can be seen giving him a little help for the latter in the film *Let It Be*.

Less openly derided, George Harrison (*"the quiet Beatle"*) is still sometimes regarded as a low-ranking musician by certain critics. Alongside two compositional giants, his chance to shine was hard won in the early years: *"It was the way The Beatles took off with Paul and John's songs, and it made it very difficult for me to get in. And also, I suppose at that time I didn't have as much confidence when it came down to pushing my own material as I have now"*. (May 1970).

Some of the more superficial comments about him are sometimes repeated, such as by sound engineer Geoff Emerick's about the 1966 recording of the song "Taxman", one of the first completed songs by The Beatles' youngest member: *"George had a great deal of trouble playing the solo – in fact, he couldn't even do a proper job of it when we slowed the tape down to half speed"*. (2006)

But here again, careful listening to the seven years of recording by the band reveals characteristics that are not immediately obvious at first glance. A lead guitarist from the outset, he first developed a light, almost impressionistic style, influenced by American Country & Western musicians such as Carl Perkins or Chet Atkins, whom he revered. Masked by the rhythmic profusion of The Beatles' early albums, this elusive style only really emerged in 1966, when the band stopped touring, a decision he had strongly championed, preferring meticulous studio work to wild anonymous concert halls.

Like Ringo, George had the delicate task of adapting to the multitude of Paul's and John's musical styles, constantly renewing his Folk-Rock expression and patiently seeking new ideas while giving a real unity to the ensemble. To understand him better, one can start for example by listening to the acoustic solo of "Till There Was You" (1963), and the disconcerting ease with which he played it live.

The famous opening chord of "A Hard Day's Night" (1964) on his 12-string Rickenbacker 360 guitar, the first magical arpeggios of "Ticket To Ride" (1965), the rich layers of acoustic guitar on "You've Got To Hide Your Love Away" (1965), the raging tones of his Gibson SG on "Paperback Writer" or "And Your Bird Can Sing" (1966) are just a few of his fantastic soundscapes that can be highlighted here. Not to mention the solos recorded backwards, starting on the album *Revolver* (1966), as recalled by a young assistant at the time, Richard Lush: "*He'd play the solo normally, then we'd reverse the tape and he'd listen backwards. But creating a solo that sounded good played backwards was a laborious process (...). It really took hours*".

For Harrison, 1966 and 1967 were essentially a period of discovery of Indian music, which he had come across by chance on the set of the film *Help!*. Although he had no theoretical knowledge of Western classical music, he embarked on a serious apprenticeship in Indian classical music thanks to Ravi Shankar, a classical sitarist already renowned at the time. The traces of this fascination can of course be found as early as 1965 with his first attempt on the song "Norwegian Wood", and then more thoroughly in compositions which for the first time fused a pop expression and an Indian sensibility ("Love You To", "The Inner Light", "Within You Without You").

George's conscious decision to focus on the guitar in 1968 for the double 'White' album consecrated him as a fully-fledged composer thanks to magnificent melodies such as "While My Guitar Gently Weeps" or "Piggies", followed in 1969 by

"Here Comes The Sun", "I, Me, Mine" or "Something", which finally earned him his first A-side of a Beatles single.

More than anything else, it was George's contribution to the overall "Beatles sound" that can best pay tribute to his significance: a guitarist with a light, lyrical style, attracted by exotic sounds and slide guitar skills, an excellent technician, a flexible and innovative musician (he also introduced the first Moog synthesizer on The Beatles' album *Abbey Road* in 1969). He was one of the major components of the band's sonic atmosphere, as Andy Babiuk, an expert in Beatles instruments, testifies: "*When you listen to the*

draft recordings of some of the songs, they're barely passable. If they had left them as they were, would they have become the hits we know and love? That's where George played such an important role".

George and Ringo in 1969

Here again, any musician who has ever tried to play a Beatles song knows that nothing is more deceptively simple than the techniques and styles of Ringo Starr and George Harrison.

10 – "The Beatles revolutionised music."

> *"Their chords were outrageous, just outrageous,
> and their harmonies made it all valid. ... That was
> obvious. ... I knew they were pointing the direction
> of where music had to go."*
>   Bob Dylan, 1971

From June 1962 to August 1969, The Beatles recorded
the bulk of their commercially released work, more
than 200 songs in 12 LP albums, 13 EP records and 22
singles. In their early days, sound engineers were
still required to wear a tie and studio technicians
wore white coats, forbidding anyone from touching
electronic equipment and closing the studio doors
after 6 p.m., as if it were an office. By the end of these
seven years, the world of music was no longer the
same, and the media landscape itself had changed
profoundly, in part thanks to The Beatles.

A typical Beatles session at Abbey Road Studios in 1964

One of the first findings that will come as a great
surprise to popular music neophytes is the fact that
the famous studios where The Beatles recorded

almost all of their output– then simply called EMI Studios and now called Abbey Road Studios – suffered from certain technological limitations in comparison with their American counterparts, which The Beatles themselves often bemoaned. But it was undoubtedly those restrictions that, from the outset, pushed them towards greater inventiveness and boundless creativity, rooted in their personal demands, as summed up by their producer George Martin: *""What kept The Beatles head and shoulders above everyone else is that they were prepared to change, do different things. No one record was a carbon copy of another"* (1995, Coleman).

Anecdotally, Paul McCartney complained for a long time that he couldn't get a really thick bass sound on their recordings, until 1966 and the "Paperback Writer" sessions. On that day, according to their engineer Geoff Emerick: *"Paul played a different bass, a Rickenbacker. Then we boosted it further by using a loudspeaker as a microphone. We positioned it directly in front of the bass speaker and the moving diaphragm of the second speaker made the electric current"*. It is also common knowledge that the entire *Sergeant Pepper's* album was recorded in 1967 on a modest 4-track tape recorder, a technology that most home musicians nowadays would regard as far too limited.

The technical innovations invented by The Beatles and their engineers are in fact so numerous that the list would be too long for this book, although most of them have become absolutely commonplace today: The deliberate use of feedback – that unwelcome piercing sound that comes from the sound loop between microphones and amplifiers (in "I Feel Fine", 18 October 1964) – the invention of the *flanger* – the addition of a slightly detuned signal to the original signal ("Tomorrow Never Knows", 6 April 1966) – the strange placement of microphones in front of drums or inside water jars, the use of sound loops, sampling, backward recordings, or even cutting up recording tape and splicing it back haphazardly, as well as countless other technical or sound effects... The Beatles laid the foundation for what studio work would be for the next decades and still is today.

Freed from the constraints of live performances after the summer of 1966, they were able to give free rein to their imagination, shattering the musical boundaries of the time. And although they were not always the first to experiment with a new technique, they were certainly the ones who did the most to popularise it, knowing how to adapt it to their music and to make it acceptable to the general public.

At the same time, a new Pop-Rock culture was born, less centred on the ephemeral singles and EPs and more oriented towards the composition of homogeneous albums. Brian Wilson, the thinking head of the Beach Boys, recalls on this occasion hearing the album *Rubber Soul* for the first time in 1965: "*I really wasn't quite ready for the unity. It felt like it all belonged together. Rubber Soul was a collection of songs... that somehow went together like no album ever made before, and I was very impressed*"

The year 1967 witnessed the birth of a new kind of recording, sometimes called a little pompously "concept albums", even if the idea was sometimes pure autosuggestion and certainly not a deliberate choice on the part of the musicians. But the overall quality of music production during this period was so high that the record industry was quick to notice and to take advantage, a shift that was greatly facilitated by the emergence of "classic rock" radio stations in the mid-1960s, particularly on the FM band, which was then in its infancy.

George Martin and Norman Smith in late 1963 with the Beatles

Driven by their curiosity and the proficiency of their regular producer, George Martin, or of their sound engineers – including the experienced Norman Smith and a very young Geoff Emerick – they continued to look for more sophisticated arrangements based on new sounds, new instruments, or changes in keys or in time. The list of Beatles' musical innovations adopted by their contemporaries and heirs also remains so obvious that it could easily be taken for granted and overlooked. How could we forget that they were the first (or almost in some cases) to use a string quartet ("Yesterday", 1965), or a sitar ("Norwegian Wood", 1965), to stop touring and favour recording (1966), to combine Indian and Rock music ("Love You To", 1966 or "Within You, Without You", 1967), to print the lyrics of their songs on an album (*Sergeant Pepper's*), to send to the top of the charts a seven-minute song ("Hey Jude", 1968) and a double album (the 'White' album, 1968), to name but a few of their innovations.

Situations that are commonplace in studios today, such as building a soundscape around a harpsichord, an English horn, a string quartet or a sitar, can largely be attributed to The Beatles, but the list is so long that one would fall asleep reading it... And all the while they maintained a formidable ability to compose seemingly simple melodies that were immediately memorable and have stood the test of time.

But technical innovations were not the only improvements brought on by The Beatles in the 1960s. Even before the start of their career, they had something no other band had: they wrote their own songs, words and music. Of course, they were fortunate enough to find in John and Paul some of the most gifted melodists of their generation, but it was above all in the constant renewal of their musical and writing styles that their genius transpired: spurred on by their new friendship with Bob Dylan, they turned to more elaborate lyrics in 1965, combining nostalgia ("Yesterday", 1965), philosophy ("Nowhere Man", 1966), psychedelia ("Lucy In The Sky With Diamonds", 1967) and politics ("Revolution" or "Blackbird", 1968). The reflections were also more personal, especially in Lennon's work ("Help!", "You've Got To Hide Your Love Away" or "In My Life", 1965), although "There's A Place" in 1963 and "I'm A Loser" in 1964 already displayed more intimate reflections.

The influence of The Beatles on the music of that era and the decades that followed can also be measured in terms of the famous musicians who openly admired their musical output. Who else could boast the unconditional support of musicians as different as Bob Dylan, James Brown, Ray Charles, Bjorn Ulvaeus (co-founder of Abba: "*The Beatles are the reason we started writing songs"*), Slash (former guitarist with Guns N' Roses: *"It's a band that completely changed the world*") or Robert Fripp (co-founder of King Crimson: *"The Beatles achieve probably better than anyone the ability to make you tap your foot first time round, dig the words sixth time round, and get into the guitar slowly panning the twentieth time"*)

Beyond these musical considerations, one final question remains: were The Beatles simply satisfied with following passing fads or did they themselves shape a lifestyle that influenced an entire generation? Let us start by leaving aside their haircut, copied by countless bands since the 1960s, including the Rolling Stones, the Ramones, etc. If no one can say for sure which band or song invented psychedelic music (although "Tomorrow Never Knows" in 1966 is a very serious contender), no one can deny that they did it with infinite talent to turn this new strand of music into an art accessible to the general public; this period also remains symbolised by the famous *Sergeant Pepper's* jackets, variations of which can still be found in fashion boutiques today.

At the same time, it was they, and more particularly George Harrison, who initiated the fascination for India and a certain taste for oriental mysticism, which would quickly turn into an increased interest in the music of Ravi Shankar, transcendental meditation or more simply yoga. It was also they who launched the first record company whose primary goal was not profit (Apple Corps, May 1968). And it was of course John Lennon who became one of the most committed activists of the pacifist cause from 1969 onwards, taking advantage of the media coverage of his wedding with Yoko Ono to invent his famous "bed-ins" against the Vietnam War.

Whatever one thinks of their music, it is undeniable that The Beatles greatly changed studio practices. But their influence on an entire generation, and on many of their heirs, goes far beyond mere technical and musical issues. It is no coincidence that they are still the group with the highest number of record collectors in the world, and that they are among the very rare musicians from the sixties whose records are still sold today at the same prices as recent albums.

11 – "The Beatles are the biggest record sellers of all time."

> "Music is everybody's business. It's only the publishers who think people own it."
> John Lennon, 1970

The figure of one billion records sold worldwide by The Beatles is sometimes mentioned by EMI, their record company, although this has never been officially proven or denied. The record sales of all artists are indeed very difficult to determine for several reasons. The first of these is the lack of exact references for a very large number of countries: While Western countries and some Asian countries keep a relatively accurate record of sales figures, this is far from being the case in many African countries, for example, from an international point of view.

Additionally, even for countries with reference agencìes, like the USA or in Europe, these were only created at the end of the 1950s, and it is extremely difficult to take into account sales prior to this period. This is particularly the case for Elvis Presley's first records, one of the few – along with Michael Jackson – to be in the same league as The Beatles.

Thirdly, each country accounts for sales on its market in its own way, and often only partially. For example, the British music weeklies *New Musical Express*, *Record Mirror* and *Melody Maker* started publishing their first sales rankings as early as 1952, 1956 and 1958 respectively. But since 1969 the main professional reference in the UK has been the magazine *Record Retailer* (renamed *Music Week* in 1972). For the USA, one of the most important and reliable markets in the world, the first figures provided by the RIAA (Recording Industry

Association of America) only date from 1958. And even with these, the sales of the large companies are only estimates and represent approximately 85% of the official market. In other words, even for the most reliable countries, sales figures until the late 80s were based on speculations with incomplete data.

Since 1991 the USA has also benefited from Nielsen Soundscan figures which seem more accurate and reliable, since they are transmitted electronically by the sales outlets and cover 95% of the official market. These figures are also used for the famous *Billboard* magazine's sales ranking. But of course, all these data do not take into account streaming services like Spotify, Deezer or Qobuz, that are probably the main listening source for younger generations, let alone illegal downloads: in November 2013, anti-piracy company MUSO discovered that The Beatles were the most-pirated artist in the world, far ahead of any other artist. According to them, illegal Beatles files were downloaded on average 190 million times per year (*Music Week*, 8th November 2013).

The only way to achieve a comparison between the serious international contenders (Elvis Presley, The Beatles and Michael Jackson) is therefore to extrapolate from the estimates provided by these relatively reliable countries.

For the USA, the oldest certified figures, those of the RIAA, thus indicate a total of about 183 million records sold for The Beatles since 1962, about 146 million for Elvis Presley since 1954 and about 84 million for Michael Jackson since 1964 (including his period with the Jackson Five).

Beyond the USA, another international body created in 1933 called the IFPI (International Federation of the Phonographic Industry) also federates the interests of record companies or national institutions: the BPI in the UK, the RIAJ in Japan, the SNEP in France or the BVMI in Germany, etc. However, its estimates are based on rankings rather than on certified sales. Its spokesman, Adrian Strain, had to admit to his great shame in 2009 *"when we were asked how many albums Michael Jackson had sold, we were quite embarrassed. And we had to turn to the Guinness Book of Records"*... Since 1971, the Guinness rankings have officially considered The Beatles as the best-selling artists of all time, citing the figure of one billion records sold since 1985, *"a total never equalled by any other artist"*, for which Ringo Starr received a Diamond Award on behalf of The Beatles at the 2008 World Music Awards ceremony.

However... all the figures mentioned above are seriously challenged by Elvis Presley fans since they are based on an equation that seems unfavourable to him: Sales are generally counted in "singles equivalents", where an EP (or maxi-single) is worth two units and an album is worth six units. But Elvis mainly sold singles, not albums...

If you really enjoy your maths, another solution is then to compare the number of singles and albums in the charts. In this case, the figures are easier to obtain

Billboard, April 4, 1964

and we can once again take as an example the USA where, according to their respective record companies, Elvis makes 60% of its worldwide sales and The Beatles 40% of their sales: between 1956 and 1977, Elvis had 19 singles and 7 studio albums at the top of the American charts; between 1963 and 1970, The Beatles had 21 singles and 17 studio albums at the top (including five songs at the top five of the American *Billboard* charts on 4 April 1964, which has never been repeated since); finally, between 1971 and 2009, Michael Jackson had 12 singles and 5 albums at the top. Once again, The Beatles come on top.

But again, Elvis or Michael Jackson fans will not be satisfied with this information, as advocates of the former will vehemently point out some flaws in the calculations: first, some of the King's albums have never been accounted for by his record company, RCA (apparently to save them from paying sales tax); and second, archival research to document all his sales is still underway. For their part, fans of the King of Pop will point out just as vehemently – and rightly so – that "Thriller" is the best-selling album of all time, with around 100 million legal copies worldwide.

A final attempt could consist in basing our ranking, not on quantitative assessments, but on qualitative values according to criteria established by recognised experts. This is what the journalists of the American magazine *Rolling Stone* tried to do in 2005, by ranking the "500 best albums of all time". Of the top 15, there are five albums by The Beatles, two by Bob Dylan, and one by Elvis Presley with his first opus (*The Sun Sessions*, in 11th place). Michael Jackson's first appearance is in 20th place (*Thriller*).

Obviously, such rankings are highly subjective and the mere title "*best albums of all time*" verges on the grotesque when you realize the listing consists essentially of Anglo-American Rock music of the last 60 years, dismissing international artists as phenomenal as Oum Kalsoum in Egypt, Ravi Shankar in India, to name but two.

The first conclusion that can be drawn from these speculations is that definitive sales figures for Elvis, The Beatles Michael Jackson, etc. will never be known for certain. The second conclusion, on the other hand, is that The Beatles certainly made a lot of money from their music. And yet...

In 1962, Brian Epstein had a hard time getting a recording contract for his *protégés*. With no legal training whatsoever, he cheerfully approved the contract proposed to him by Parlophone (a subsidiary of EMI) on June 4, 1962. McCartney admitted many years later, "*Brian turned to his father to learn how to run his business, and his father knew how to run a furniture shop in Liverpool*".

The 4-page contract, valid for one year, specified that The Beatles would be paid for sales in the UK *one penny* per song (1/240th of the old pound sterling, used until 1971, i.e. around 7 pence of today's money), and half of that figure abroad. Each album with 14 songs (like most of their British albums from 1963 to 1966) generously paid them seven old pence (i.e. £0.50, or $0.65, today) – to be divided by four, of course!

This agreement was renewed three times, and EMI prolonged it until it expired in 1966, at the end of which Brian Epstein demanded a revision that finally saw their royalties increase dramatically after January 1967. Until then, The Beatles had been content with receiving a weekly salary and letting the money flow into their accounts: but in 1967 The Beatles realized the value of founding their own company, which they did with Apple Corps in 1968, thus sealing a joint partnership. Driven by the same wind, their loyal producer George Martin had already left EMI in 1965 to found his own production company, AIR.

Another source of income for The Beatles was copyright, mainly for Lennon and McCartney. The Northern Songs company was formed in 1963 with the help of their manager Brian Epstein and an advisor, Dick James, and was floated on the stock market in 1965. John and Paul each owned 15% of the company and received their annual dividends and royalties.

But here again, trouble was on the way: after Epstein's death in 1967, Dick James gave up his 15% share to the ATV television channel without warning the two main authors, who were legally obliged to continue their collaboration as a pair until 1973. Under these conditions, the best way out for them was to sell their shares and abandon their dividends, while continuing to collect their royalties.

But in 1985 the enormous ATV catalogue was again put up for sale and bought for around 47 million dollars by Michael Jackson, mainly thanks to the royalties he had received for the single "The Girl Is Mine", recorded three years earlier as a duet with... Paul McCartney! In 1995, the catalogue was subsequently merged with Sony's, and Michael Jackson agreed to sell half of his share in 2006 to settle his debts. Sony/ATV now owns 75% of the old Northern Songs catalogue, while McCartney has managed to buy

Paul McCartney and Michael Jackson, 1982

back four of his first songs from a catalogue that predates Northern Songs. He is also very proud to have bought Buddy Holly's catalogue in 1976, not as a prudent investor, but as a long-time admirer.

A final source of income came from merchandising, although the term had not yet been coined at the time. As early as 1963, Brian Epstein had been looking for someone to take care of this side of the business, which was of very little importance at the time, since artists generally had a short life span and were not profitable in this respect. Stramsact (for the UK) and Seltaeb (for the USA), were immediately a huge success under the leadership of Nicky Byrne, who demanded and obtained 90% of the profits in return. Epstein soon realised his mistake and after a few months was offered a revised contract and 49% of the profits. Epstein then sued Byrne for not accounting the sales properly and cancelled the deal, which led to a counter-suit that lasted for 3 years, and which he lost. By that time, most companies had lost any interest and this undoubtedly played a significant role in his depressed periods, convinced that the four Beatles would never forgive him and would not renew his contract as their manager in late 1967.

It is of course very easy, almost 60 years later, to mock Brian Epstein's professional shortcomings and lack of business sense. Yet, The Beatles' success can be attributed to a large extent to Epstein's contacts in the industry and sensible handling of the group's image. It is also critical to remember that, as his assistant Alistair Taylor noted in his 2002 autobiography, "*We did our best; some people have said it wasn't good enough. That's easy to say with 20/20 hindsight but remember that there were no rules. We were making it up as we went along*".

12 – "The Lennon-McCartney rivalry broke up the group."

> *"I never wanted The Beatles to be has-beens, I wanted to kill it while it was on top."*
> John Lennon, *Hit Parader* magazine, 1972

The cooperation between John Lennon and Paul McCartney is regarded as one of the finest examples of twentieth-century musical partnerships, while its epilogue is certainly one of the most saddening. Born of their chance meeting at a parish fête in Liverpool on 6 July 1957, their friendship blossomed over the next twelve years, only to disappear in the autumn of 1969.

Along many other reasons, this ultimate breakdown in communication can be explained by the personalities of the two protagonists: John was impulsive and refused to compromise; Paul was controlling and probably anxious. For years, the group operated in a totally collective, even fusional way: Until 1966, their extraordinary creative energy fuelled by their studio work can largely be attributed to this core musical tandem. As early as 1963, the two songwriters had reached an agreement to credit both names for their songs recorded with The Beatles, regardless of each person's contribution: This was the birth of the famous "Lennon-McCartney" seal of approval, formally recognised by the creation of two publishing houses, "Northern Songs" for the UK (1963) and "MacLen" for the USA (1965), which would go on to publish around 180 of their songs.

The Lennon and McCartney symbiosis was undoubtedly the main source for the group's inventiveness and stylistic diversity, driven by an emulation and complementarity that has rarely been equalled: "*In 'We Can Work It Out,' Paul did the first half, I did the middle-eight. But you've got Paul writing, 'We can work it out/We can work it out' --real optimistic, y' know, and me, impatient: 'Life is very short and there's no time/For fussing and fighting, my friend'...*" (Lennon, *Playboy* interview, 1980).

But as years went by, this flourishing cooperation gradually gave way to more explicit differences in style. Not very intense at first, they slowly and naturally revealed a more personal approach to their respective musical developments from 1965 onwards. Their compositions became more intimate, and it is widely known for example that only Paul McCartney took part in the recording of the song "Yesterday" on the album *Help!* (August 1965).

From 1966 onwards, starting with the album *Revolver*, and even more prominently in *Sergeant Pepper's* (1967), their work became even more complex, and the writing more elaborate. Still, some sort of cooperation remained, clearly perceptible in the collage song "A Day In The Life", probably the most beautiful example of their collaborative work. This individualisation naturally led to a weakening of the band's homogeneity: 1968 even saw Ringo momentarily leaving the band during the 'White' album sessions, apparently due to a lack of recognition from the other members of the band. Of course, the media were left in the dark, and Ringo quickly returned to the studio, finding his drum set decked out with flowers offered by George.

John & Paul, 1968

January of the following year got off to a very bad start with the recording sessions for the film *Let It Be*, when Harrison once coldly responded to the slightly authoritarian McCartney, during a very tense session: "*I'll play whatever you want me to play, or I won't play at all if you don't want me to play. Whatever it is that'll please you, I'll do it.*" It was now his turn to leave the band for a few days, before eventually returning with pianist Billy Preston, whose presence encouraged everyone to remain on their best behaviour throughout the remaining sessions.

The musical gap between the two writing partners further widened in 1968 with John's meeting with Yoko Ono. Within a few weeks, the Lennon-McCartney musical partnership gave way to entirely individual and sometimes avant-gardist recordings, such as "Revolution 9", which was imposed by John on the last side of the 'White' album.

McCartney was not opposed to experimental recordings, on the contrary. But their new ways of composing now left far less room for collaboration, although in May 1969 Paul gave John a great deal of help in the studio with the recording of "The Ballad of John and Yoko", while George and Ringo were absent.

Although their musical styles had by then already begun to diverge, a real sense of shared purpose still gave some unity to their artistic production. From 1968 on, a deeper difference in purpose and ambition slowly emerged, as Paul explained later: "*When we started off we were all aiming for pretty much the same thing. I think the troubles really began when we weren't aiming anymore for the same thing, which began, I think, when we stopped touring in 1966*" (*Life Magazine*, 1971).

The swan song came with the next album, recorded in the summer of 1969 despite the growing artistic dissensions: "*By the time we made Abbey Road, John and I were openly critical of each other's music and I felt John wasn't much interested in performing anything*

*he hadn't written himself (...) So I felt the split coming.
And John kept saying we were musically standing
still."(Life Magazine, 1971).* Never short of ideas, Paul
suggested in September 1969 that they head back to
the stage to play some improvised concerts in small
halls and clubs. John replied in his usual offhand
manner "*You're daft*", and then added, "*anyway I'm
leaving the group, I want a divorce, like with my wife
Cynthia.*"

Beyond musical considerations, financial issues
were yet another cause of dissension between
Lennon and McCartney. While Ringo and George
never interfered with Paul and John's artistic
relationship, things were quite different concerning
financial and legal matters. And in 1969, Paul found
himself alone against the other three band members:
John had met the Rolling Stones' manager Allen
Klein, an American businessman who was willing to
defend their financial interests against EMI.
Impressed by his track record, John managed to
convince George and Ringo to sign an agreement
with him in May 1969. In the autumn, Ringo advised
Klein not to divulge to the public the final separation
requested by Lennon while negotiations were still
underway with their record company.

Paul, for his part, had not signed the agreement,
preferring to be represented by Lee and John
Eastman, American lawyers and relatives of his new
wife. Up until that time, any member of the group
could veto a decision that he deemed inappropriate,
but in late 1969 a legal division appeared for the first
time.

Then, in early 1970, Paul forced EMI to postpone
until May the release of The Beatles' album *Let It Be*
to prioritise the release of his first solo album in
April. This was accompanied by a pseudo-interview
in which he announced that he no longer had any

joint projects with the other Beatles because of *"personal differences, business differences, musical differences"*.

This announcement was a bombshell for the music world, even though Paul was merely publicising a situation that, for the last eight months, had been acknowledged behind closed doors by every member of the band. But the fact that he was the first to publicise the split added to the resentment felt by John, George and Ringo. John in particular could not forgive Paul for using the separation to draw public attention to the release of his first solo album. In response to a short reference by McCartney in a song (*"Too many people preaching practices (...), That was your first mistake, You took your lucky break and broke it in two"* in "Too Many People", 1971), Lennon wrote one of his cruellest, and almost laughable invectives: *"Those freaks was right when they said you was dead (...) The only thing you done was yesterday / The sound you make is muzak to my ears (...)/ How do you sleep at night?"* ("How Do You Sleep?", 1971).

Eventually, the two men more or less reconciled during the last few years of John's life and Paul later recalled his last telephone conversation with him: *"I do feel it was sad that we never actually sat down and straightened our differences out. But fortunately for me, the last phone conversation I ever had with him was really great, and we didn't have any kind of blowup"* (*Playboy* interview, 1984).

13 – "Yoko and Linda were responsible for the separation."

> "The Beatle thing is over. It has been exploded, partly by what we have done, and partly by other people. We are individuals-- all different. John married Yoko, I married Linda. We didn't marry the same girl."
> Paul McCartney, *Life Magazine*, 1969

Unlike Maureen Cox, Ringo's first wife (1965-1975), or Pattie Boyd, George's first wife (1966-1974), Yoko Ono and Linda Eastman, wives of John and Paul respectively, have been accused of accelerating, or even causing the group's break-up.

Yoko first appeared in John Lennon's life at an exhibition at the Indica Art Gallery in London in November 1966. Of Japanese origin and a member of the avant-garde movement Fluxus, Yoko seemed to be completely unaware of the world's most famous Pop-Rock band, allegedly not paying any particular attention to the musician at first. It wasn't until early 1968 on returning from a trip to India that Lennon finally divorced his first wife, Cynthia Powell, and married Yoko Ono in Gibraltar on 20 March 1969.

Paul McCartney first met American photographer Linda McCartney in New York in May 1967 while still being in a relationship with the then young actress Jane Asher. After the relationship ended, Paul and Linda began living together in September 1968 and were married in London on March 12, 1969, a few days

before John and Yoko. Their first daughter Mary was born in August 1969.

It was therefore during this period of turbulence within the group that two of the main members found their muse, but in very different ways. Linda was already a well-known photographer, with a portfolio that included work with the Rolling Stones, Jim Morrison, The Who, Jimi Hendrix, among others. It was in this context, and after a previous failed marriage, that she was sent on a mission to London by the American magazine *Rolling Stone* to cover the launch of the Beatles' album *Sergeant Pepper's...* in May 1967. A few months later, it was she who shot the four portraits inserted in the 'White' album sleeve.

Coming from a family of American lawyers, she was then unwillingly involved in messy legal issues plaguing the group when Paul chose her brother and father to defend his own financial interests. John, George and Ringo on the other hand chose Allen Klein, rightly considering that hiring Paul's in-laws would give rise to a conflict of interest.

From this period onwards, Linda became Paul's one and only muse: after years of flings and affairs, he had finally decided to settle down to a quiet family life, and the press booklet inserted in his first solo album in April 1970 explained Linda's contribution: "*Strictly speaking she harmonizes, but of course it's more than that because she's a shoulder to lean on, a second opinion, and a photographer of renown. More than all this, she believes in me – constantly.*" At first the main criticisms she had to respond to in the early seventies, was having cut Paul off from social life and the media. Very soon, there was also much taunting and mockery when Paul decided to teach her to play the keyboard and to compose, in order to become a full member of his new band, Wings.

But gradually, Linda McCartney managed to regain the public's esteem, especially thanks to her friendly and unassuming attitude in the media but also, in no small way, thanks to her range of vegetarian products, greatly appreciated in the British Isles: her death from cancer in April 1998 was without any doubt one of the severest blows her husband ever took. Uninvited to the funeral by Paul, Yoko explained in May 1998 in the magazine *Rolling Stone* the resentment of the band's fans towards her and Linda in the late sixties and seventies: *"Then came The Beatles breakup. The world blamed Linda and me. I think the fans needed scapegoats and they chose us."*

The grievances against Yoko Ono are, however, of a completely different nature, and many agreed with the group's official biographer, Hunter Davies when he wrote: *"If there is only one reason for the separation, it is the arrival of Yoko"*. Weakened by several years of intense touring and recording, Lennon was in 1968 in an exploring and introspective phase focusing on his insecurities, which at first pushed him towards drugs. His encounter with Yoko was a powerful catalyst, as John never did things in half measures and always embraced new adventures wholeheartedly.

The fact that Yoko was now John's girlfriend did not pose any particular problem in itself, as Paul recognised in 1995: *"I can't blame him, they were madly in love"*. But the primary source of conflict within the band in the very first months was obviously her omnipresence. There had  been until then an unspoken rule that friends or spouses did not attend nor participate in recording sessions: Yoko Ono, on the other hand, never left Lennon's side, even when recording, and the underlying tension was described by George in 1995: "*At first it was a novelty, but after a while it became apparent that she was always going to be there and it was very uncomfortable (...), there was a definite vibe, and that's what bothered me. It was a weird vibe.*"

Of course, her presence at Abbey Road was entirely motivated by John's own wish, and the tensions reached their peak in early July 1969 when he demanded a bed for a convalescing Yoko in Studio 2. In a 1998 television interview, their producer George Martin still remembered this episode bitterly: "*There was a period when she was ill, and John insisted that her bed be set up in the studio so that she could rest there and watch us record, and that's not the best way to make a record*".

In addition, John also wanted Yoko to have her say in the musical creation of the band. This desire regularly led Yoko, a classically trained pianist, to give her opinion on The Beatles' musical choices and arrangements, sometimes provoking the ire of the other members of the group. Mark Lewisohn, the eminent historian of Beatles recording sessions, notes in one of his very rare subjective remarks that "*Yoko attended every Beatles recording session and would encourage hostility by whispering conspiratorially into John's ear, by sitting on his amplifier and appearing to preside over the session, by openly criticising and suggesting changes*".

Finally, Yoko has sometimes been criticized for supposedly setting her sights on John from the beginning, perhaps to benefit her own career as an avant-garde artist. For, while John tended not to take himself seriously and had fun making avant-garde recordings, this was not the case for Yoko, for whom fame was a goal in itself. She explained to journalist Marshall McLuhan in 1969: "*I wasn't working with anybody before that. Always doing things myself. And somehow I find it easier now (…). And, of course, John has much more access to communication, you know, and all that. So, we're using that".* But while defending herself from having precipitated The Beatles' break-up, she also justified this natural evolution of things shortly afterwards, not without a certain common sense: *"If the four of them had gone on, then they would have suffocated each other."* (Hit Parader, 1972).

Ever since 1976, a marginal but recurring dispute on the Lennon-McCartney signature has also seen bitter arguments developing between Paul and Yoko. This concerns the official order of names, especially for titles such as "Yesterday": having written and recorded the song without the other three Beatles, Paul logically felt the credits should officially be changed to "McCartney-Lennon", which Yoko Ono has always refused. But the tension seems to have eased a little over the last decades, and they sometimes can be seen together, as on the occasion of the announcement of the video game The Beatles - Rock Band in 2009.

The media world is now looking forward to reading Yoko Ono's memoirs, which she has mentioned several times in her interviews although they still remain to be written: when she is ready, these will perhaps explain why John's first son with Cynthia Powell – Julian Lennon, born in 1965 – is so often 'forgotten' in official documents that she has sanctioned. He was thus completely left out of his father's will in 1980 for reasons that only lawyers can understand, and is regularly removed from his father's official biographies, as in 2006 in Paris for the Lennon exhibition at the Cité de la Musique.

If the impact of Linda and Yoko was certainly noteworthy in the relationships within the band from

1968 onwards, the proper reasons why they decided to part can be found elsewhere: the death of their manager Brian Epstein, the musical and artistic differences, George Harrison's status in the band, legal and financial problems, etc. These were the real factors that revealed the artistic and personal differences between the four individuals, pushed to the limit by the fusional relationship between John and Yoko, but also by Paul's passion for Linda.

On a positive note however, Linda and Yoko both enabled their husbands to give up drugs and to shed themselves of the personae imposed on them by the media, which they had been trying to do for some years. As for Yoko, she can also be credited with having always championed the cause of world peace with her newfound notoriety, or with having opened her husband's eyes to feminist issues. Paul himself admitted a few years later: "*He wanted fresh challenges all the time. So it was nice of Yoko to fulfil that role. She gave him a direction*" (*Playboy* interview, 1984). As for John, he beautifully summed up his thoughts on the subject: "*If it is Yoko and Linda's fault for breaking up The Beatles, can they have the credit for all the great music that each of us have made individually?*" (1971).

14 – "The post-Beatles era: legal actions galore."

"People said, 'It's a pity that such a nice thing had to come to such a sticky end.' I think that too. It is a pity. I like fairy tales. (...) But you realize that you're in real life, and you don't split up a beautiful thing with a beautiful thing."
McCartney, *Life Magazine*, 1971

On April 10, 1970, Paul McCartney issued a press release announcing his first solo album and declaring that he no longer had any common project with the other members of the group: this marked the official end of The Beatles for the media and for the general public. On December 31 of the same year, on his lawyers' advice, he reluctantly began legal proceedings against the other three members to dissolve The Beatles entity and regain his artistic independence. Since then, numerous lawsuits surrounding the group have followed one after the other, be it within the Apple Corps entity, against the EMI record company or against Steve Jobs' Apple Inc. brand.

The first procedure, launched in 1970, lasted until 1977 and saw Paul battling the trio John-George-Ringo. The origin of this initial dispute dated back to 19 April 1967, when The Beatles had signed a partnership without paying too much attention, binding them for 10 years under the name "Beatles &

Co". In 1968, The Beatles' Apple Corps became an 80% partner, with the remaining 20% divided into four 5% shares. In addition, John and Paul were under contract until 1973 with the Northern Songs company, which published all their songs.

Fascinated by one of John's statements in an interview with Ray Coleman in January 1969 ("*if it carries on like this, all of us will be broke in the next six months*"), Allen Klein – the American manager of the Rolling Stones from 1965 to 1970 – managed to convince three of The Beatles that he could help them. Paul, on the other hand, chose to hire his in-laws, John and Lee Eastman, as managers. However, a contract was signed on 9 May 1969 between Klein and his three supporters, with Paul missing. After some initial success in his American negotiations with Capitol Records – where he obtained new and much more favourable copyright conditions for The Beatles – it became clear that Klein was not the most honest of managers. This was evidenced for example by his 1971 conviction in New York for tax evasion and the subsequent lawsuit brought against him by John, George and Ringo in 1973.

Meanwhile... George Harrison was under attack for plagiarism for his song "My Sweet Lord" (1970), considered too similar to the 1963 Chiffons hit "He's So Fine". The song was now Allen Klein's property as part of the Bright Songs catalogue, and in 1976, he was found to have committed "sub*conscious plagiarism*". This trial inspired him to write a new song, simply entitled "This Song", in which he sang "*This tune has nothing Bright about it*" and "*This song don't infringe on anyone's copyright.*"

So it was first and foremost Allen Klein who was targeted in Paul's 1970 lawsuit, as the ex-Beatle was now essentially trying to regain his artistic freedom: the 1967 contract stipulated that any project by one of the four, even solo, had to be approved by the other three. McCartney explained for example to the judge how shocked he was by Phil Spector's arrangements of his song "The Long and Winding Road", as stated in his very firm letter of 14 April 1970 to Klein: "*In future, no one will be allowed to add to or subtract from a recording of one of my songs without my permission (...) Don't ever do it again*".

Other issues, far less concerned with artistic matters, were also discussed during this trial, which found its epilogue after many years of negotiations: John was sued twice, first by Klein, then by Northern Songs (1973). John counter-attacked with George and Ringo against Klein (1973), and the partnership of the four Beatles was finally dissolved (31 December 1974), although the Apple Corps entity still remained in order to defend their common interests.

On 10 January 1977, a global financial agreement between Apple and ABKCO (Allen Klein's company) put an end to all legal action between the parties involved, but the damage was done: Paul was now seen by the media and the general public as the one who had put an end to the dream of the sixties and had taken his former partners to court.

Meanwhile… John was threatened with deportation from the US because of a 1968 conviction for marijuana possession in Britain: in 1973, he began a long legal battle to obtain a residence permit, only receiving his green card in 1976, allowing him to reside permanently in the U.S.

Between 1973 and 1982, EMI – along with Capitol for the USA – published a long series of Beatles compilations: after obtaining their agreements to publish the "Red" and "Blue" albums in 1973 (officially called *1962-1966* and *1967-1970*), it went on, this time without prior consent, to release *Rock'n'Roll Music* (1976), *The Beatles at the Hollywood*

Bowl (1977), *Love Songs* (1977), *Rarities* (1978), *Reel Music* (1982) and *20 Greatest Hits* (1982). Weary of their insufficient influence over these releases, The Beatles requested a financial audit of EMI-Capitol in 1979 through Apple, essentially in order to verify the veracity of the sales figures and to obtain damages of 20 million dollars.

And meanwhile... Paul McCartney tried in vain to buy the Northern Songs catalogue of Lennon-McCartney songs, which was later bought by Michael Jackson.

It was against this backdrop that EMI and Capitol first released The Beatles' complete catalogue of their British albums in 1987 on CD, but in mediocre quality. The following year, the band was inducted into the Rock'n'Roll Hall of Fame, in the presence of George, Ringo and Lennon's widow, Yoko Ono. Paul, on the other hand, chose to abstain and issued a brief statement: "*After 20 years The Beatles still have some business differences which I had hoped would have been settled by now. Unfortunately, they haven't been, so I would feel like a complete hypocrite waving and smiling with them at a fake reunion*".

This business dispute temporarily ceased in 1989 when EMI granted the group an increase in royalties and promised that The Beatles sales accounts would now be more transparent. By now, fans had come to realize that The Beatles catalogue was nothing else than a golden goose for EMI-Capitol, probably the most precious of all, and that the quality of the recordings now released was not their main concern. For this very reason, Apple Corps was able to prevent the release of a double box set of the band in 1991 thanks to a court decision.

And meanwhile... Apple was also suing American multinational Nike (1987), guilty of having used the song "Revolution" for an advertisement without its agreement.

Hostilities resumed in 2005, when Apple demanded £30 million ($59 million at the time) in compensation from EMI-Capitol for unpaid royalties. For the first time, they also wanted to recover all the group's tapes, jealously hidden by EMI in a secret vault. In April 2007, a confidential agreement between all parties was reached out of court, which paved the way for the release of The Beatles' albums in fully remastered versions on 9 September 2009 (09/09/09). A Rockband video game dedicated to their music was also released, aimed at attracting a new generation.

While the release was once again heralded as a landmark event by the general public (more than two million CDs were sold in the first five days, almost forty years after the band had split up!), many fans couldn't help thinking it had been a long time coming, for a result that fortunately lived up to their high expectations.

Additionally, a series of sombre and lasting lawsuits between Steve Jobs' Apple Inc. and The Beatles own Apple Corps meant that The Beatles remained far too long among the few major artists whose music was not available to download legally on the internet, especially on the iTunes platform.

The first of these lawsuits, between 1979 and November 1981, saw the computer company Apple Inc. pay damages and promise never to venture into the music business, while Apple Corps promised never to diversify into the computer business.

This agreement was first challenged when Apple Inc. was one of the first, in 1986, to implement a sound card and MIDI functions on its computers, allowing recent synthesizers to be remotely controlled. The Beatles' company logically considered this novelty as a musical function, in violation of the 1981 agreement. Accordingly, their lawyers even half-jokingly suggested Steve Jobs rename his company Banana or Peach if he wished to pursue its development in the musical field. Finally, an agreement signed in October 1991 allowed Apple Inc. to continue making computers with musical functions in return for a $26 million compensation and on condition that it would never use its name and logo for *"creative works whose main content would be music"*.

But the music imperative was so ambiguous that Steve Jobs' lawyers became worried when the designers of the new OS7 system for Apple computers decided to associate different sounds with actions such as powering on or clicking – a practice that is commonplace today but was extremely innovative at the time. So frightened was Steve Jobs in fact, that sound engineer Jim Reekes jokingly announced that the start-up sound would be called "Let It Beep". He later changed his mind and finally named it "Sosumi", a fake-Japanese title whose provocative meaning was quite clear to everyone in the company: *'So, sue me!'*. It is still there in your sound library if you have a Mac, and is still called "sosumi.aiff". At Apple Corps, nobody noticed the pun.

Steve Jobs in 2010

A fragile peace between the two companies had therefore been signed, which lasted for more than ten years. But in 2001, Apple launched its famous iPod audio player, followed in April 2003 by its online music platform, iTunes. Apple Corps sued again for breach of the 1981 agreement, but in May 2006 the judge ruled in favour of Steve Jobs' Apple Inc. A confidential agreement was finally reached between the two parties in February 2007.

Meanwhile, Steve Jobs could declare, "*My business philosophy was inspired by a band, the Beatles: My model for business is the Beatles. They were four guys who kept each other's kind of negative tendencies in check. They balanced each other, and the total was greater than the sum of the parts*" (*60 Minutes* interview, 2003).

In this new and peaceful context, nothing prevented The Beatles from being distributed online... except their financial and artistic demands: Apple records were looking for an exclusive distribution agreement in exchange for a very large sum of money. Despite the complexity of the situation (between EMI who own the recordings, Sony-ATV who own the publishing rights, and Apple Corps who represent The Beatles), an agreement was finally concluded in 2010. Once again, legal complications had seen The Beatles missing the innovation train, they who during the 1960s had been at the forefront of cultural and technological originality...

15 – "The Beatles' solo careers have been dismal."

"I still love those guys. The Beatles are over, but
John, Paul, George and Ringo go on."
John Lennon, *Playboy* interview, 1980

Between the break-up in 1970 and the assassination of John Lennon in December 1980, hopeful rumours of secret meetings between the four former Beatles members to hold a reunion spread around the globe. These rumours were particularly rife in 1976, when two American promoters offered them respectively $50 million and $230 million for a single charity concert. Rather embarrassed by their ongoing lawsuits and not in the least interested in the money, they logically rejected both offers.

But the ex-Fab Four continued to collaborate throughout the 1970s on their solo albums. The four acolytes can for instance be heard on the drummer's album *Ringo* in 1973, albeit on different songs. This record was a phenomenal commercial success in both the United States and Great Britain, perhaps the only real solo success for Ringo Starr in his very prolific post-Beatles production.

Although Ringo's solo career is generally regarded as rather insignificant by most commentators, one of his distinctive traits is of course that he does not take himself too seriously. And so he continues to record albums full of nostalgia exploring his own celebrity status

with humour, relying on collaborations with his show business friends, from Eric Clapton to Elton John, Jeff Lynne, Quincy Jones, David Gilmour, Brian Wilson, etc. That being said, Ringo Starr is the only ex-Beatle to have had a real acting career, especially during the 1970s.

By contrast, Paul McCartney has enjoyed a particularly rich and varied commercial career since 1970, albeit somewhat inconsistent. His first albums in particular are often described by critics as unfinished attempts or as sophisticated productions lacking real intensity: *Ram* and *Wild Life* in 1971, or *Red Rose Speedway* in 1973 both come to mind in this respect. And it was probably these initial disappointments that turned the 1973 album *Band On The Run* into such a welcome surprise, so much so that even today it is still as McCartney's most creative and cohesive album, recorded with his then-new band, Wings.

 This collective period lasted for six years with some highs (the top-selling single "Mull of Kintyre" in 1977, McCartney's first top-selling single since The Beatles) and some lows (*Wings at the Speed of Sound* in 1976) before ending with two solid melodic albums: *London Town* (1978) and *Back to The Egg* (1979).

McCartney's next solo phase was based in great part on duets, for what was probably the most kitschy period of his career: first with Stevie Wonder in 1982 ("Ebony and Ivory"), then with Michael Jackson in 1983 ("The Girl is Mine" for the Album *Thriller*, and "Say, Say, Say").

It then took ten long years for him to bounce back and for his fans to rediscover him at his best, thanks to a significant collaboration with Elvis Costello for *Flowers in the Dirt* (1989). Following his comeback Between 1990 and 1996, he released only one studio album and devoted much of his musical time to The Beatles' *Anthology* project (1995-2000), which saw the publication of a documentary series and three double set-boxes, including two new Beatles tracks based on old demos by John Lennon.

McCartney's successful collaborations continued with Jeff Lynne in 1997 (*Flaming Pie*), also considered as one of his best albums, followed by recordings of Rock'n'Roll covers (*Run, Devil, Run* 1999) produced shortly after the death of his wife Linda (1998). A new somewhat disappointing period (*Driving Rain* in 2001) was finally overcome thanks to a cooperation with producer Nigel Godrich in 2005 (*Chaos and Creation in the Backyard*), followed by a largely self-produced and critically acclaimed album (*Memory Almost Full*, 2007). More recently, only *Egypt Station* (2018) has enjoyed real success, giving him his first number one album in the US since 1982.

It is generally agreed that Paul's melodies can occasionally be naive, that his lyrics can lack intensity and that his prose may at times verge on the overly sentimental: all of these make the absence of artistic emulation – which was evident when composing with John – cruelly felt in a production deemed somewhat below his former standards. But it would be difficult (to say the least) to find anyone else in the music business with such an extraordinary career: in 60 years, he has received 60 gold albums all over the world, and written or co-written 129 songs that have cracked the *Billboard* Top 100, 43 of those selling over 1 million copies. In his solo career alone, he has recorded 25 studio albums and 9 live albums, with artistic forays into the world of techno-ambient music (such as 'The Fireman' in 1994, 1998 and 2008) or into classical music (from *Liverpool Oratorio* in 1991 to *Ocean's Kingdom* in 2011). One would be hard pressed to find a better track-record than this.

 John is undoubtedly the ex-Beatle who composed the most intense individual body of work, as much for its brevity (1969-1980) as for the nature of the themes addressed. Jon Landau, music critic and producer, analysed the divergent paths followed by the Liverpool Four as follows: "*Of the four former Beatles, John Lennon and George Harrison have gone on to write exclusively in the first person, their lyrics, both good and bad, never more or less than simple statements of their ideas and feelings. Ringo Starr and Paul McCartney have moved in the other direction, expressing themselves no less personally but through more inventive means*"(*Rolling Stone* magazine, January 1974).

Leaving aside his three experimental productions with Yoko Ono in 1968 and 1969, Lennon's solo career began before The Beatles split up with three singles, including "Give Peace A Chance" associated with his campaign for peace in the summer of 1969. The 1970 album *Plastic Ono Band*, his first and perhaps best opus, channelled his frustration and rage for life during a dark period of intense psychological introspection: the song "Mother", which opens the album, is perhaps the most cathartic of all, while "Working Class Hero" is pure Lennonian sarcasm, and "God" attempts to close the utopian sixties trance with its famous line: "*I don't believe in Beatles (...) the dream is over*".

In the great tradition of a John Lennon who spent his life searching for himself – and often contradicting himself – this eloquent idealism can be found on his next album and on his single "Imagine" (1971), which remains to this day his most lasting success. Adopted by many pacifist movements, it has been heard on the radio so often that one could end up getting tired of it, despite its obvious merits as a powerful and much needed anthem for peace. In parallel with this pursuit of universality, this period of personal reconstruction also enabled Lennon to write such gems as "Jealous Guy" (to a 1968 tune), as well as a violent diatribe against McCartney, "How Do You Sleep?".

The following years were marked by a production greatly varying in quality, hitting rock-bottom with his double political manifesto *Some Time In New York City* (1972), recorded with his wife Yoko. Strangely enough, only the albums recorded during their two-year separation (*Walls and Bridges* in 1974, and *Rock'n'Roll* in 1975) seemed to revive the creative capacities he had previously enjoyed, before they reunited and he chose to become a 'househusband', looking after his second son Seán.

The final episode of John Lennon's career, however, (*Double Fantasy* in 1980 and the posthumous sequel *Milk and Honey* in 1984) remains a mystery: how ironic that his rage and sarcasm had given way to a rose-coloured musical style he had so often derided McCartney for! What can explain his total lack of musical discernment in letting Yoko Ono write and record half of the tracks? Confused by this ultimate production, most fans simply admit that love can make one deaf.

George Harrison's early career was surprisingly similar to that of John Lennon: in 1969, he also released an album of experimental music before turning to the same producer – the famous Phil Spector – to record what is still considered his best album, the triple *All Things Must Pass* (1970). Seeing The Beatles' separation as a real chance to express

 himself, he developed a unique style based on light Pop-Blues melodies and inimitable guitar sounds. He also tended throughout this period to openly display his lifelong religious convictions for Hare Krishna, notably in his most famous single "My Sweet Lord" (1971).

The rest of his solo career was also a musical roller-coaster, with obvious disappointments (*Somewhere in England*, 1981; *Gone Troppo*, 1982) as well as great achievements: after a five-year hiatus due to frustration, *Cloud Nine* (1987) was the last studio album published during his lifetime, produced with Jeff Lynne, Ringo Starr, Eric Clapton and Elton John. In addition to the hit "Got My Mind Set On You" – a cover of an obscure 1962 James Ray song – George succumbed once again to nostalgic temptation with "When We Was Fab", also a hit single. After his death from cancer in 2001, a final posthumous album was released by his son Dhani and Jeff Lynne in 2002 (*Brainwashed*), which was also very well received by critics.

Beyond music, George was also the inventor of charity concerts (*The Concert for Bangladesh*, 1971), as well as the main financier of the first Monty Python film (*Life of Brian*), an enlightened racing car enthusiast, and one of the five members of the Traveling Wilburys (with Roy Orbison, Tom Petty, Bob Dylan and Jeff Lynne), who released two albums in 1988 and 1990.

It should therefore come as no surprise that there is no common measure between The Beatles' solo careers and their former achievements as a unit: the genuine interaction of four musical geniuses on a single record will always be more compelling than the dispersion of their talents.

But in their defence, while their separation after seven years of intense collaboration in the studio gave them greater creative freedom, it also enabled them to evade decline, which would have naturally occurred sooner or later. Additionally, public and media expectations were extraordinarily high in 1970 and they had to reinvent themselves, but this time individually: to a certain extent, they invented the concept of a solo career, which could not be based on any precedent of individual musical success after phenomenal collective success.

Conclusion

> "The real point is, there are only four people who knew what The Beatles were about anyway. Nobody else was in that car with us."
> Paul McCartney, *Playboy* interview 1984

In addition to the criticisms sometimes directed at The Beatles' music, a number of unsympathetic voices have asserted that they were simply lucky enough to arrive in the USA eight weeks after John F. Kennedy's assassination, during a period when the whole nation's spirits were extremely low. This is undoubtedly true. Recent criticisms consider, also correctly, that The Beatles became famous for changing the world, but are now paradoxically revered as classics, in a rather conservative and rigid way. This appears to be confirmed even by one of the most conservative institutions of all, the Vatican, in its official organ the *Osservatore Romano*: "*Thirty-eight years after the break-up of the group, the songs of Lennon and McCartney have shown an extraordinary resistance to the passage of time, becoming a source of inspiration for more than a generation of pop musicians*" (21 November 2008). Four decades after their scandalised reaction to Lennon's claim that they were "*more famous than Jesus*"... Better late than never!

The fact remains that – over fifty years after their separation – they still enjoy considerable airtime on radio stations all over the world, can sell records in massive quantities at the same prices as current artists, conquer new audiences with each passing decade, and are cited as an absolute reference by the greatest artists. In addition to Oasis, whose admiration for the Fab Four verged on obsession, artists such as Radiohead, the Pixies, Nirvana and the Foo Fighters, Lenny Kravitz, Blur, Gorillaz, Lady Gaga, Shakira, Ed Sheeran, Lewis Kapaldi and many others have claimed The Beatles legacy.

The sheer density and homogeneity of their body of work thus remains a source of inspiration on many levels, and sales continue to prove it: the success of the *Anthology* CD box sets in 1995 (855,473 copies sold in the first week of release in the US alone) confirmed their relevance to music critics and the general public alike. In 2009, after more than twenty years' waiting for good quality releases of The Beatles' official CDs (dating back to 1987), fans welcomed EMI's decision to release the entire official catalogue in remastered versions on 9 September 2009 (09/09/09), with more than 2 million copies sold in one week in the USA, Great Britain and Japan alone.

Again in 2010, the band sold more than 450,000 albums and 2 million individual songs in their first week on iTunes, thanks to a vast marketing campaign. More recently, Ron Howard's documentary *Eight Days a Week* won the Grammy Award for Best Music Film in 2017, three major Beatles albums were released in deluxe and remixed versions for their 50th anniversary (*Sgt Peppers...*, the 'White' album, and *Abbey Road*) and have topped the charts, while movies such as *Yesterday* by Danny Boyle (2019) carry on the process of endearing The Beatles' magic to the children of the 21st century.

There is absolutely no doubt today that The Beatles have become part of the Western artistic heritage, as evidenced by the very strong public and media reaction in February 2010 when EMI announced its intention to sell Abbey Road Studios – before retracting its announcement a few days later as a result of the outrage.

The 20th century will thus go down in musical history as the period when two Western traditions merged – classical and popular music – largely thanks to The Beatles. Unfortunately, few artists have taken up the torch: music based on the strength and simplicity of Rock, pushed to a level of inventiveness and experimentation meant to break artistic and social barriers while remaining extremely popular worldwide. This was summarised in direct terms in 2004 by Howard Goodall, film-score composer and author of a British television series on music theory: "*The incredible diversity and richness of style of their music is one of the reasons why they are much more than just another 60s pop band*".

To conclude, I would also like to add a personal opinion: As a teenager, I remember proclaiming in a serious discussion with adults that people would still listen to the Beatles in the 21st century. Some of the listeners laughed. I now have no doubt that, not only will The Beatles remain major composers and musicians of the 20th century, but their music will still be played in the 22nd century by our great-grand-children.

ADDITIONAL INFORMATION

Bibliography

Close to 10,000 books have been written about the Beatles and it is simply impossible to cite only a small number of those without forgetting others. So here is a small selection, entirely subjective, none of them making any claim to perfection. The first part is meant to help beginners, and the second part those who would like to go a little further.

For beginners

The best book – but one of the most expensive – on the history of the group is undoubtedly *The Beatles Anthology* (2000), consisting almost entirely of extracts from interviews with the four musicians, and some of their close professional entourage. A television documentary series under the same name was also broadcast worldwide in 2000.

Another interesting approach is to read their biography, but opinions differ wildly among fans on which book best describes the band's history and context.

Among the most important works are: Hunter Davies' *The Beatles: the authorised biography* (2009), Nicholas Schaffner, *Beatles Forever* (1977, 2nd ed. 1997); Philip Norman, *Shout! The Beatles in Their Generation* (1981, 2nd ed. 2004); Bob Spitz, *The Beatles: The Biography* (2005). Mark Lewisohn has also started writing the most accurate biography to date, but only the first volume has been published so far: *Tune In: The Beatles: All These Years* (2013).

For individual biographies, one might be interested in Barry Miles' *Paul McCartney: Many Years from Now* (1998) or Philip Norman's *Paul McCartney: The Biography* (2017).

John Lennon's biographies are abundant but two stand out: Philip Norman's *John Lennon: The Life* (2009) and Ray Connolly's *Being John Lennon* (2019). Of course, John also wrote two books in the 1960s, in the British nonsense genre: *In His Own Write* in 1964, and *A Spaniard In The Works* in 1965.

Only George has written his own (very short) autobiography, with Derek Taylor: *I, Me, Mine* (1980, 2nd ed. 2008). A more comprehensive approach is given in Simon Leng' *The Music of George Harrison: While My Guitar Gently Weeps* (2002) and in Graeme Thomson's *George Harrison: Behind The Locked Door* (2013).

Fewer books have been written about Ringo, but Alan Clayson's *Ringo Starr: A Life* (2005) and Michael Seth Starr's *Ringo: With a Little Help* (2015) are regarded as the best way to understand The Beatles' drummer.

For fans

Among the most interesting documents written by the Beatles' entourage, the memoirs written by their manager Brian Epstein in 1964 is a must read, despite its very superficial character (*A Cellarful of Noise*). More interesting are George Martin's memoirs *All You Need is Ears* (1979, 2nd ed. 1994) and Geoff Emerick's (with Howard Massey) *Here, There and Everywhere: My Life Recording the Music of the Beatles* (2007).

Concerning the end of their career and the history of Apple Corps, one should read Denis O'Dell's book with Bob Neaverson, *At the Apple's Core: The Beatles from the Inside* (2003).

Also worthy of mention are Bill Harry's *The Beatles Encyclopedia: Revised and Updated* (2000); Peter Brown and Steven Gaines, *The Love You Make: An Insider's Story of The Beatles* (2002); Cynthia Lennon, *John* (2006).

More specialised works include: Roy Carr and Tony Tyler, *The Beatles: An Illustrated Record* (1975, 2nd ed. 1981); Kevin Ryan and Brian Kehew, *Recording The Beatles* (2006); Andy Babiuk, *Beatles Gear: All the Fab Four's Instruments, from Stage to Studio*, (2001, 2nd ed. 2010); Kenneth Womack, *Winding Roads: The Evolving Artistry of the Beatles* (London, Continuum IPG, 2007); Ian MacDonald, *Revolution in the Head: The Beatles' Records and the Sixties* (London, Vintage, 1994, reprinted 2008).

Finally, Mark Lewisohn deserves a special mention with *The Complete Beatles Recording Sessions* (1988, 2nd ed. 2004), *The Beatles Day by Day: A Chronology 1962-1989* (1990) and *The Complete Beatles Chronicle* (2000, 2nd ed. 2013).

Discography

Complete beginners will probably wish to start with two compilations: *1962-1966* (The "Red" album) and *1966-1970* (the "Blue" album), initially released by Apple in 1973.

If you wish to listen to the complete collection, remastered versions of the original recordings were released in September 2009 – i.e. the 12 original British albums, one American album, and two compilations of their singles. Additionally, three Beatles albums (*Sgt Peppers...*, the 'White' album, and *Abbey Road*) have been released in deluxe and remixed versions for their respective 50th anniversary between 2017 and 2019.

Here is the complete list, with those in bold being considered as the most important:

- *Please, Please Me* (1963)
- *With The Beatles* (1963)
- ***A Hard Day's Night* (1964)**
- *Beatles For Sale* (1964)
- *Help!* (1965)
- ***Rubber Soul* (1965)**
- ***Revolver* (1966)**
- ***Sergeant Pepper's Lonely Hearts Club Band* (1967)**
- *Magical Mystery Tour* (1967, US version)
- ***The Beatles* ("white" album) (1968)**
- *Yellow Submarine* (1969)
- *Let It Be* (1970)
- ***Abbey Road* (1969)**
- ***Past Masters 1 & 2* (1988 compilations)**

The *Let It Be* album was also revisited in 2003 under the name *Let It Be... naked*, without Phil Spector's heavy production, following Paul McCartney's wishes.

For lovers of rare or alternative recordings, *The Beatles Anthology* collection includes three exciting double albums.

For those who would like to listen to almost everything, here is a complementary list, some albums being sometimes sold under different names:

- *1962 Live At The Star Club In Hamburg* (double album, historical recordings, but only for real amateurs since the sound is clearly lo-fi);

- *The Beatles In The Beginning* (studio recordings in Hamburg in 1961 with singer Tony Sheridan);

- *The Lost Decca Sessions* (recorded on 1 January 1962 for Decca, who turned them down);

- *Live At The BBC* (double album, live recordings at the BBC from 1962 to 1965);

- *Live At The Hollywood Bowl* (only official concert recordings, in 1964 and 1965 in Hollywood).

- Finally, a remix album entitled *Love* was released in 2006, containing the soundtrack of the *Cirque du Soleil* show of the same name in Las Vegas.

Other recordings such as studio rehearsals and outtakes, live performances or home demos – called bootlegs – are not available commercially.

Among the many documentaries about The Beatles, Howard Goodall's *Twentieth Century Greats: Lennon & McCartney* (broadcast in November 2004 on Channel 4 in Great-Britain) stands out as an excellent analysis of the musical genius of the band's two main composers.

Websites

- *www.thebeatles.com* – official website.

- *www.johnlennon.com* – *www.paulmccartney.com*, *www.georgeharrison.com* – *www.ringostarr.com* – official websites of the four members of the group.

- *www.brianepstein.com* - official website of their manager Brian Epstein.

- *www.georgemartinmusic.com* – official website of their producer George Martin.

- *www.abbeyroad.com* – official website of the EMI studios.

- *www.beatlesinterviews.org* – an impressive database of radio, press and TV interviews.

- *www.beatlesbible.com* – a remarkable fansite, by Joe Goodden.

- *https://bit.ly/342Fx5L* – advanced musicological analyses of the songs, by Allan Pollack.

- *wgo.signal11.org.uk/wgo.htm* – "What Goes On?" an analysis of audible anomalies in the songs, by Mike Allen.